CONTENTS

		Page
	Dedication and Acknowledgements	iv
	List of illustrations	vi
	List of tables	vii
	List of abbreviations	viii
	Introduction	1
Chapter 1	'The Shrieking Sisterhood': The Suffrage Question in Angus	9
Chapter 2	From Suffragists to Citizens	15
Chapter 3	Arbroath 'Women Citizens'	23
Chapter 4	'Filling a Need': AWCA Work 1931-1945	41
Chapter 5	Committee Women: The Scottish Council of Women Citizens' Associations	52
Chapter 6	Conclusion: The Politics of Daily Experience	57
	Epilogue 1	61
	Epilogue 2	63
	Appendix 1	64
	Appendix 2	65
	Bibliography	72
	Index	78

DEDICATION

This publication is dedicated to all 'women citizens' in Scotland for their commitment to their local communities and for carrying out important work, which went unnoticed by many.

ACKNOWLEDGEMENTS

I have been extremely fortunate in having been offered help from many people who have always been very generous with their time and I would like to thank all who have been involved with this project. In particular I wish to thank Mrs Caroline Florence and Mrs Main of the current Arbroath Women Citizens' Association who have, on numerous occasions, welcomed me into their homes and with much patience have answered my endless stream of questions about the Association. For enquiries into Forfar, Mrs Findlay and Mrs Ada Cochrane proved of great assistance in providing background information. Mrs Lind was also a wealth of information on the Forfar branch and it is to my regret that she passed away during my research and never saw the end result. Sincere appreciation must also be given to Brian Forsyth at the Arbroath Herald who gave me access to the newspaper's archive. Jane Milroy also supplied information on former secretary of the group, Annie Ellis. Dr Norman Watson and Dr Sue Innes not only made very helpful suggestions for locating material on the topic but also more importantly offered me encouragement. I also wish to express gratitude to the library staff at Forfar, Arbroath and the University of Dundee and the archive staff in Angus and the National Archives of Scotland. I also wish to thank Dr Elspeth King, the Arbroath Herald and Angus Archives for very generously agreeing to have pictures reproduced in this publication.

I have attempted to locate all copyright holders of material that appears in this publication. If material appears without copyright permission, this has occurred because I have been unable to locate who the copyright holder is.

The basis of this publication came from research I undertook as an undergraduate student for my dissertation at the University of Dundee. It went on to win the Abertay Historical Society prize in 2004 and for this I must thank Dr William Kenefick who believed in my assurances that this was a viable research topic and was of great help as supervisor. More generally, the history department at the University of Dundee have always been very supportive of my research initiatives and my current supervisor, Professor Callum Brown, must also be thanked for not only challenging the way I view and write history but also for at all times offering me encouragement. I am also very grateful to my family who have supported me throughout my studies.

This publication would never have come to fruition had it not been for the Abertay Historical Society. In particular I wish to thank Matthew Jarron, General Secretary of the Abertay Historical Society for his guidance. Indeed, the entire committee of the Abertay Historical Society have all been most helpful with this project. I am also very grateful to Dr Kenefick who edited the manuscript for this publication and offered much appreciated ideas for improvements. I also wish to express gratitude to The Strathmartine Trust who have generously covered some of the costs of this publication. Final thanks must go to the women of the Arbroath Women Citizens' Association without whose careful preservation of their records this research would never have been completed.

Sarah F. Browne, 2007

LIST OF ILLUSTRATIONS

		Page
Plate 1	Suffragettes At Forfar – Reproduced with permission from Dr Elspeth King.	33
Plate 2	Flora Drummond – Reproduced with permission from Dr Elspeth King.	33
Plate 3	Suffragette Caravan, 1913 – Reproduced with permission from Angus Council Cultural Services.	34
Plate 4	Mrs Amy Sanderson, 1910 – Reproduced with permission from Dr Elspeth King.	35
Plate 5	Suffragettes at Brothock Bridge c. 1911 – Reproduced with permission from the Arbroath Herald.	36
Plate 6	Arbroath Women Citizens, 1931 – Reproduced with permission from the Arbroath Herald.	37
Plate 7	Syllabus Card 1937-1938.	38
Plate 8	Front cover of Scottish Council of Women Citizens' Associations handbook.	39
Plate 9	Women Citizens North East Area Conference – Reproduced with permission from the Arbroath Herald.	40
Plate 10	Arbroath Women Citizens' Association Work Party.	40

LIST OF TABLES

		Page
Table I	Membership Numbers of Arbroath Women Citizens' Association during 1931-1945.	30
Table II	Proportion of Arbroath 'Women Citizens' in relation to population in Arbroath and Dundee.	31

LIST OF ABBREVIATIONS

Arbroath Women Citizens' Association (AWCA)

Business and Professional Women's Federation (BPW)

Dundee Women Citizens' Association (DWCA)

Edinburgh Women Citizens' Association (EWCA)

Forfar Women Citizens' Association (FWCA)

National Union of Societies for Equal Citizenship (NUSEC)

National Union of Women's Suffrage Societies (NUWSS)

Scottish Council of Women Citizens' Associations (SCWCA)

Women Citizens' Association (WCA)

Women's Co-operative Guild (WCG)

Women's Freedom League (WFL)

Women's Liberation Movement (WLM)

Women's Social and Political Union (WSPU)

Women's Voluntary Service (WVS)

Young Women's Christian Association (YWCA)

INTRODUCTION

In 1928, Ray Strachey, a prominent Suffragist, stated that 'the records of the women's movement are easily accessible and most of the events are still within living memories'.[1] Yet almost eighty years later this situation has declined to such an extent that few historical documents of the post-suffrage women's movement survive. The reason why this situation has so badly deteriorated is of less consequence than actually attempting to preserve what still remains. The papers of the Arbroath Women Citizens' Association (hereafter AWCA) are one such surviving archive and ensuring its preservation is the main justification of this study.

This is part of a wider problem relating to historical sources and which in part explains the deficit from which the writing and promotion of women's history suffers. Clearly contributing to this situation, as Lynn Abrams has observed, is that 'the story told of Scottish history is very much man-made', and that historians of women and gender in Scotland have been disappointed by the marginalisation of the experience of women in Scottish history.[2] The experience of women in Scotland was thus overshadowed by masculine concerns, but a further problem was that it was also subsumed within a much broader literature on women's history in Britain. Viewed from this perspective, as Sue Innes asserted, 'Scottish women have been doubly hidden from history'.[3] A further and leading contributory factor is that women's history developed comparatively late in Scotland when compared to other countries, and this was due to an over-reliance by the academy on political history.[4] Put simply, Scottish political history has been 'an exclusively male domain.'[5] There therefore needs to be a widening of the definition of the 'political' in Scottish history in order to give fuller recognition, and to gain a greater understanding, of the role of women in the political process. Yet this is by no means a uniquely Scottish phenomenon. Considered within a European context, for example, Karen Hunt recently described how there has been a 'peculiar inscription of masculinity on the subject' and that by focusing on what was termed 'high' politics, the role of women was relegated to something of a sideshow.[6] This suggests an obvious third layer in terms of the deficit from which Scottish women's political history suffers, for not only are they less visible for being women, and for being Scottish, but also because campaigning groups such as the Women Citizens' Associations (WCA) are not included in discussions of the conventional 'high' politics of Parliaments and elections.[7] This publication should be seen as a contribution to this development in questioning what can be termed as the 'political' in Scottish history. It is essential, therefore, in order to cast more light on the work of groups such as WCAs, that there must be a shift in emphasis that favours a historical examination of the campaigning work done by the majority of women and not simply the political endeavours of an exceptional minority.

Whilst it has been correct to isolate three layers of deficit within Scottish women's political history, the preliminary findings of this study suggest a fourth layer. Some historians, for example, assert that groups such as the WCA advocated a very limited agenda and promoted a fairly restrictive programme of activity. The agenda of the WCAs was thus regarded as quite distinct from the more 'militant' campaigns of the Suffragettes and Women's Liberation Movement (WLM).[8] As the suffrage and WLM campaigns were very much image-centred, with great emphasis placed on the role of political propaganda, they have come to dominate the literature on women's political history. Indeed, some historical works would suggest that after the suffrage campaign effectively ended in the 1920s, 'feminism appeared to have died', and thereafter their activities were put on hold until campaigning resumed once again in the 1960s and 1970s.[9] Brian Harrison noted in *Prudent Revolutionaries* that this was perhaps inevitable because 'historians, like journalists relish the dramatic, the flamboyant, the outrageous'.[10] Such a limited approach works very much to the detriment of the WCA and discounts and ignores the campaigning activities they pursued over the intervening period.

This study points to the importance of the WCA network to the history of Scottish women, but notes too that research in this field of women's history in Angus is particularly problematic. This is mainly due to the simple fact that there is a lack of historical literature on Scottish women generally and more specifically on the experience of women in Arbroath. This trend has been somewhat reversed in recent years and an important 'turning point' in this development came with the publication of *The World is Ill-Divided* and *Out of Bounds* by Eleanor Gordon and Esther Breitenbach. These books stimulated new research into nineteenth and twentieth century women's history, but from the outset they make it clear that there is a 'paucity of publications on the history of women in Scotland'.[11] They have played a crucial role in re-establishing the important contribution made by Scottish women to the historical record and in reclaiming women's history, but only in passing do they make any significant reference to the WCA. Another important publication for women's history in Scotland was Leah Leneman's seminal work *A Guid Cause*, which drew attention to the fact that the study of the suffrage movement is by no means an exhausted subject and that there was still much to discover about its impact on Scotland.[12] R. K. Marshall also published *Virgins and Viragos* which placed the women's movement in a much broad historical context, but only includes a very short piece on the workings of the Edinburgh WCA (EWCA). Further interest has been stimulated more recently by the publication of the edited collection *Gender in Scottish History Since 1700*, and significantly *The Biographical Dictionary of Scottish Women*. Both of these publications have brought Scottish gender research up to date and they also utilise the latest gender theories to explore further themes in Scottish women's history.

It should be noted that this area in historical study has not been entirely neglected, and in relation to the inter-war women's movement in particular, historians such as Olive Banks, Barbara Caine and Harold Smith have sought to promote the role of women. Underpinning much of the literature on this topic, and in the context of the inter-war period, is the debate which focuses on the nature of 'old' and 'new' feminism, and the differences between each school of feminist thought. Old feminism was in essence the pre-war (1914-18) political movement based on political struggle, whilst new feminism was a strand of feminist thought, popularised in the immediate aftermath of World War One, that placed more emphasis on women as wives and mothers than the equal-rights tradition thought necessary.[13] It was the impact of new feminism, however, which has come to dominate the historiography of the women's movement after 1918, and in general terms this debate has focused on whether new feminism was a particularly helpful development for women. Susan Kingsley Kent, for example, argued that it 'limited their ability to advocate equality and justice for women'[14] - believing it to have championed rather than challenged pre-conceived notions of gender. Views such as these have characterised new feminism as helping 'to buttress an essentially anti-feminist ideology'.[15] This has led some historians, such as Angela Holdsworth, to suggest that 'the romantic struggle for the vote had been replaced by dreary committee work'.[16]

Whilst these arguments do indeed have merit, Harrison would stress that the political context has to be considered as feminists shifted their beliefs for political opportunity and became, in a sense, 'prudent revolutionaries'.[17] Further attempts to neutralise the criticism directed at new feminists have argued that they were moving away from purely defining equality simply on men's terms.[18] In addition that far from limiting women to the private sphere it gave 'all women a choice'.[19] What most historians of this subject have neglected to look at in detail, however, is the work of the WCAs.[20] It is reasonable to suggest, therefore, that the historiography would clearly benefit from research in this area, especially in light of Norman Watson's conjecture that they (the WCA) 'repeatedly crossed the divisions in competing feminist theories'.[21]

Two important and guiding influences in this study derive from unpublished Ph.D theses. The first was produced by Sue Innes, who charted the developing ideas of feminism and citizenship during the period 1900 to 1939. In order to illustrate many of her points she examined the papers of the EWCA and in concluding, her analysis confidently claimed that this body was 'an ambitious autonomous women's organisation active at a time when feminism is believed to have been in almost terminal decline'.[22] The second thesis was by Norman Watson who analysed gender and politics in Dundee, 1870-1977. In undertaking this research he looked at materials relating to the activities of the Dundee WCA (DWCA), and in conclusion remarked that it was clear that there was very little research on this and other such organisations 'in relation to political activity and their bearing on feminist theory'.[23]

Noting the gaps in historical knowledge identified by Innes and Watson - and using much unpublished evidence - this study advances five main objectives. The first is to preserve the archive of the Arbroath WCA and document the workings of a group which is still prominent in the community today (over the past years so much women's history has been lost, and there was a real and genuine concern that the AWCA material could have met with a similar fate). The second aims to examine the AWCA as an organisation - which is perceived to have incorporated new feminism into its ideology – in order to ascertain whether the neglect of this nation-wide body on the part of historians means that female political campaigning during this period must now be judged in a very different light. The third aims to move the focus of the study beyond the main cities of Scotland and establish how gender issues affected smaller urban centres using Arbroath as a case study. The fourth objective seeks to challenge a leading historiographical argument - and a common misperception - that the women's movement ended political campaigning by 1928. Finally, this investigation aims to contribute to the wider developments taking place in gender studies by reconceptualising the notion of the 'political' in Scottish history.

In order to achieve these objectives this study will be divided into chapters - arranged thematically - to highlight how the women's movement evolved in the aftermath of the suffrage campaign. The first chapter will set the topic in a wider historical context and will concentrate largely on the suffrage movement in Angus, in order to show that there was a long history of women willing to campaign for the cause of equal citizenship. By adopting a comparative approach that considers the activities of the EWCA and the DWCA, this study will further demonstrate that there were close links between the WCA and local suffrage organisations, and a further general comparison of WCA activity in Angus will seek to highlight a similar link. While these connections may not have been apparent in all cases the main aim of chapter one will be to examine this question from a somewhat different perspective and consider to what extent the suffrage movement helped politicise women and in turn encouraged them into establishing and participating in other organisations such as the WCA. Chapter two will look at this development in greater depth, focusing both on national politics and the local political considerations in Arbroath. The evidence presented here not only points to the existence of a flourishing women's movement locally but that many national trends and strands of feminist thought were reflected in the activities of women in Arbroath.

Chapter three will provide a general summary of the procedure used for the creation of a WCA and its associated national body in order to promote a greater understanding of their work, and to demonstrate how their society functioned and operated. The main aim of this chapter is to consider the establishment of the WCA in Arbroath, and based on an analysis of residential addresses, provide a membership profile of that body. This will show that the membership was middle class, but more importantly that at a time when most historians believed women's lives were dominated by issues germane to the domestic sphere, these women displayed a drive and ambition that was very much in evidence in the public sphere. In addition, this chapter will reconstruct the lives of some of the leading female personalities involved in the AWCA now largely forgotten by the community in Arbroath. Issues of class are also considered in this chapter and possible links with the labour movement are also explored. This analysis will give some indication of the diversity in the political and campaigning agenda promoted by the AWCA.

The work of the AWCA is the focus of chapter four and considers specifically the periods 1931-4, 1935-8 and 1939-45. Important AWCA campaigns will be examined such as the drive for more policewomen, the question of equal pay, and the issue of domesticity. This will offer the reader some sense of how the AWCA balanced both domestic concerns and questions of social equality in order to demonstrate how the distinctions between various forms of feminist thought could easily become blurred. This study draws to a close by examining how far feminism had declined by the 1930s by placing the study in a wider national context, and assessing the role of the Arbroath WCA in the broader Scottish Council of Women Citizens' Associations (SCWCA) based in Edinburgh.

This current study cannot be regarded as a complete account. There is still much to be done to recover what has been lost since Ray Strachey wrote her history of the women's movement in Britain in 1928. This book does, however, illustrate that if the drive and determination is there then further resources for the study of women's history will be uncovered and as Joy Hendry suggests 'history is there for Scottish women.'[24] Hopefully, this will encourage more interest and research into the inter-war women's movement by reconstructing the operation and activities of an association and its various bodies that today still remain largely hidden from history.

NOTES

[1]   R. Strachey, *The Cause: A Short History of the Women's Movement in Great Britain*, (London, 1928), p. 5.

[2]   L. Abrams, 'Writing Women Back into the History Books', *The Scotsman*, January 15 2005; L. Abrams, 'Introduction: Gendering the Agenda' in L. Abrams, E. Gordon, D. Simonton and E. Yeo (eds), *Gender in Scottish History Since 1700*, (Edinburgh, 2006), p. 3.

[3]   S. Innes, 'Preface' in L. Leneman, *Into the Foreground – A Century of Scottish Women in Photographs*, (Edinburgh, 1993), p. 5.

[4]   E. Ewan and M. Meikle, 'Introduction' in E. Ewan and M. M. Meikle (eds), *Women in Scotland c. 1100-1750*, (East Linton, 1999), p. xx.

[5]   J. McDermid, 'Missing Persons? Women in Modern Scottish History' in T. Brotherstone, D. Simonton and O. Walsh (eds), *Gendering Scottish History – An International Approach*, (Glasgow, 1999), p. 39.

[6]   K. Hunt, 'Women as Citizens: Changing the Polity' in D. Simonton (ed), *The Routledge History of Women in Europe Since 1700*, (Abingdon, 2006), p. 216.

[7]   S. Innes and J. Rendall, 'Women, Gender and Politics' in Abrams, Gordon, Simonton and Yeo, *Scottish History*, p. 44.

[8]   B. Caine, *English Feminism 1780-1980*, (Oxford, 1997), p. 239; p. 255.

[9]   This misperception has been prevalent in many historical works on this subject: for example see Olive Banks, *Faces of Feminism – A Study of Feminism as a Social Movement*, (Oxford, 1987), p. 6.

[10] B. Harrison, *Prudent Revolutionaries – Portraits of British Feminists during the Wars*, (Oxford, 1987), p. 1.

[11] E. Breitenbach and E. Gordon (eds), *Out of Bounds: Women in Scottish Society 1880-1945*, (Edinburgh, 1992), p. 1.

[12] L. Leneman, *A Guid Cause: The Women's Suffrage Movement in Scotland*, (Edinburgh, 1995), p. 1.

[13] According to much of the historiography 'new' feminists concentrated on

introducing welfare reforms in order to improve the lives of women, whereas 'old' feminists focused largely on extending equal rights for women.

[14] S. Kingsley Kent, 'Gender Reconstruction after the First World War' in H. L. Smith (ed), *British Feminism in the Twentieth Century*, (Aldershot, 1990), p. 66.

[15] O. Banks, *The Politics of British Feminism 1918-1970*, (Aldershot, 1993), p. 3.

[16] A. Holdsworth, *Out of the Doll's House: The Story of Women in the Twentieth Century*, (London, 1989), p. 191.

[17] Harrison, *Prudent Revolutionaries*, p. 7.

[18] J. Lewis, *Women in England 1870-1950 – Sexual Division and Social Change*, (Sussex, 1984), p. 104.

[19] V. Bryson, *Feminist Political Theory - An Introduction*, (London, 1992), p. 105.

[20] The only substantial references that could be found are in B. Caine, *English Feminism*, and M. Pugh, *Women and the Women's Movement in Britain 1914-1999*, (London, 2000). Both only deal with the English context and in the case of Pugh, devotes more space to the Women's Institutes and Townswomen's Guilds.

[21] N. Watson, 'Daughters of Dundee - Gender and Politics in Dundee - The Representation of Women 1870-1977' (unpublished Ph.D. thesis, Open University, 2000), p. 222.

[22] S. Innes, 'Love and Work: Feminism, Family and Ideas of Equality and Citizenship, Britain 1900-1939', (unpublished Ph.D thesis, University of Edinburgh, 1998), p. 1.

[23] Watson, *Daughters of Dundee*, p. 198.

[24] J. Hendry, 'Snug in the Asylum of Taciturnity: Women's History in Scotland' in I. Donnachie and C. Whatley (eds), *The Manufacture of Scottish History*, (Edinburgh, 1992), p. 135.

1

'The Shrieking Sisterhood':
The Suffrage Question in Angus

In the references made to the Scottish WCAs a clear link has been established between their formation and the suffrage movement. For example, both Norman Watson and Sue Innes highlight the inclusion of a number of prominent suffrage campaigners in the WCA branches in Dundee and Edinburgh.[1] Similarly, Leah Leneman has argued that 'many members of disbanded suffrage societies joined newly-created Women Citizens' Associations'.[2] In attempting to find if this link existed within the formation of the AWCA it became immediately apparent that very little had been documented on the impact of the 'Votes for Women' campaign in Arbroath and, indeed, in Angus as a whole. This seems more than a little strange when considering Leneman's assertion that Dundee was one of 'the three main centres of the Edwardian women's suffrage movement in Scotland'.[3] For the suffrage movement to have been solely contained within Dundee would be quite remarkable especially when many workers of Dundee came from the Angus countryside.[4] With such a movement of people it is hard to imagine there not also being an exchange of ideas.

Perhaps the intensity of the campaign in Dundee has tended to overshadow the efforts of those in Angus? This study has found, however, that far from being simply an extension of the Dundee campaign the suffrage movement in Angus was indeed both distinct and prolific. It would certainly appear that there is much scope for wider investigation of this topic. With just a cursory look at a selection of local and national newspapers during this period, it would appear that Angus, especially during the years 1908 to 1911, was a national focus for suffrage activity. This was mainly due to the by-election in the Liberal stronghold of the Montrose burghs in 1908, prompted by the resignation and then death of Sir Henry Campbell-Bannerman, which brought many prominent suffragists to Angus.[5] The suffragettes began proceedings in Montrose by setting up committee rooms in Bridge Street with Una Dugdale, a colleague of Mrs Pankhurst's, in charge.[6] Indeed, during this particular by-election, the local community appeared to welcome the speeches made by suffrage campaigners, with some men heard to shout 'ca awa, wifie, yer daein fine'.[7]

This initial contact encouraged further activity as within the same week Mary Gawthorpe, organiser and member of the Women's Social and Political Union (WSPU) during 1907 to 1911, addressed the workmen of the engineering works of Keith and Blackman and Douglas Fraser and Sons. During this meeting, Miss Gawthorpe distanced herself from the Unionist or Liberal candidate but advised that supporters try to keep out the Government nominee.[8] In fact 1908 was the year when the Suffragettes formally inaugurated their campaign in Arbroath by holding a public meeting in the Victoria Hall. The newspapers reported that 'a large proportion of the audience consisted of women' and that due to its popularity many people failed to gain admission.[9] This indicates that there was much interest in Arbroath surrounding the 'Votes for Women' question. Indeed, it is significant that a large proportion of the audience were women. Whether or not they agreed with the sentiment of the speeches, such a meeting could act to encourage their politicisation. The speakers at this meeting were Mrs Pankhurst and Miss Crooker, a WSPU member who had just been released from prison because of suffrage activities.[10]

Indeed, many prominent names of the suffrage campaign were frequently attracted to the Angus area such as Teresa Billington-Greig, a founder of the Women's Freedom League (WFL), when visiting Forfar and speaking at The Cross in 1907.[11] Helen Fraser, a prominent National Union of Women's Suffrage Societies (NUWSS) campaigner, also addressed a meeting in Kirriemuir in 1909.[12] Fraser frequently visited Angus on a horse-drawn caravan which travelled down the east coast from Aberdeen, through Montrose, Brechin, Arbroath, Carnousite, Forfar and down into Perthshire.[13] Flora Drummond or 'the General' as she was nicknamed, a leading figure in the WSPU, also set up headquarters in Forfar in 1909.[14] Drummond, especially, seemed to earn the respect of the local community with the *Forfar Herald* describing her as 'a vivacious little lady, brimful of enthusiasm for the cause she advocates so strenuously, and is capable of working hard and enduring much for her movement'.[15] This influx of such national suffrage personalities did not mean that local women were deterred from involvement in suffrage activities, however, as Miss F. M. Duncan of Kinnettles and a Mrs Duncan in Arbroath presided over local meetings.[16] The main local suffrage personality, however, was Amy Sanderson who appears to have been a resident in Forfar for three or four years.[17] Leneman has shown how she firstly joined the WSPU in Forfar but after the split within their ranks over the militancy question she allied with the WFL. She was an active speaker in Scotland addressing some ninety-seven meetings in 1909 alone.[18] Indeed, she was described as being 'a fluent speaker, and is in great request at social gatherings'.[19]

Her notoriety, however, came from an incident that occurred at Herbert Asquith's private residences in Cavendish Square in London during February 1908.[20] Sanderson was imprisoned at Holloway for her part in the disturbances (this form of punishment being preferred over a fine of £2 in order to maximise the propaganda impact).[21] She was sent to prison for one month with Annott Robinson, a member of the WSPU in Dundee, and fellow WFL member Anna Munro and they became known as the 'Scotch Brigade' to the prison guards and fellow inmates.[22] This incident also had national implications as Sanderson was honoured at Caxton Hall in London. The ceremony was presided over by Charlotte Despard, President of the WFL, and Sanderson was presented with the WFL's Badge of Honour.[23] Sanderson was obviously admired by those within the WFL, but the local press seemed less impressed with the *Forfar Herald* promoting the report with the banner headline 'Female Hooligans'.[24]

There seemed to be widespread disbelief at the activities of suffrage campaigners in Angus. One article referred to them as 'the shrieking sisterhood' and a group of visiting suffragettes to Forfar were even stoned by local school children,[25] and the *Arbroath Herald* likened their presence to an invasion.[26] There was, however, some support for these groups with prominent names in the Angus community backing their campaign. Mr William Warden, a J.P. in Forfar, stated that 'the settlement of the women's vote question is long overdue' and Sir George Baxter of Invereighty declared that 'I generally approve of the suffrage being extended to women'.[27]

Despite considerable suffrage activity historians of the women's movement, with the exception of Elspeth King, tend to overlook Arbroath. Indeed, King suggests that a similar situation existed in the early part of the twentieth century, noting complaints that the Suffragettes had not visited Arbroath and that the WSPU subsequently did so in 1908 after they accepted an invitation extended to them by local fishermen.[28] All of the main suffrage groups were present in Arbroath with Helen Fraser and Una Dugdale of the WSPU presiding over a large audience in the New Public Hall in 1908.[29] Open-air meetings addressed by Anna Munro of the WFL in 1908 and two hunger strikers, Alice Paul and Edith New, making an appearance at Brothock Bridge in 1909.[30]

What cannot be conclusively stated, however, is that there existed direct links between this activity and the establishment of the AWCA. Without comprehensive membership lists for the local suffrage societies there is some difficulty in being able to isolate membership crossover. A much more likely beginning for the members of this association was the Young Women's Christian Association (YWCA).[31] This was established nationally in 1877, and sought to provide activities for young working women. They welcomed the extension of the franchise but did not openly participate in the suffrage campaign due to the risk of alienating members.[32] Indeed, Catriona Beaumont states that in the YWCA 'an emphasis was placed on citizenship education' and thus it can be seen why it was such a good recruiting ground for the AWCA.[33] The YWCA appears to have been active in Arbroath from at least 1891 and they were affiliated to the local branch of the British Women's Temperance Association.[34] They carried out much local charitable work and also contributed to international campaigns such as in 1930 when they established the 'Sunshine Club' for girls in Cape Town, South Africa.[35] They clearly provided a social outlet for local women with regular social meetings for their membership, but also provided classes for the study of such things as the Bible and for skills such as sewing.[36]

The existence of both the AWCA and YWCA indicate that citizenship as a concept was a welcome development for the women's movement in Arbroath. The YWCA clearly placed an emphasis on the education of women as citizens and in many cases provided a social outlet for local women. The legacy of the suffrage campaign, however, can not be underplayed as it created an atmosphere in which women felt able to carve out a role for themselves within developing civil society. Whilst there were no obvious direct links, the suffrage movement enabled women to become politicised and begin the campaign for equal citizenship, a concept which was central to the AWCA.

NOTES

[1]   Watson, *Daughters of Dundee*, states that 'several high-profile members of the DWCA had previous experience in suffrage societies.' (p. 201)
      Innes, *Love and Work*, highlights that the 'committee was made up of women who had been suffragists and suffragettes.' (p. 160).
[2]   Leneman, *A Guid Cause*, p. 216.
[3]   L. Leneman, 'Dundee and the Women's Suffrage Movement 1907-1914' in C. A. Whatley, *The Remaking of Juteopolis - Dundee circa 1891-1991*, (Dundee, 1992), p. 80.
[4]   I. H. Adam, *The Making of Urban Scotland*, (Montreal, 1978), p. 93.
[5]   Leneman, *A Guid Cause*, p. 62. Sir Henry Campbell Bannerman resigned in 1908 due to ill health and in April died. Morley, the MP for the Montrose Burghs is transferred to the Lords by Bannerman's successor, Asquith thus leading to the need for a by-election.
[6]   The Scotsman (TS), 28 April 1908.
[7]   Leneman, *A Guid Cause*, pp. 62-63.
[8]   Arbroath Guide (AG), 2 May 1908.
[9]   AG 2 May 1908.
[10] AG 2 May 1908.
[11] Biographical information on suffrage campaigners can be found in Leneman, *A Guid Cause*, pp. 253-273.
      Leneman, *A Guid Cause*, p. 255; *Forfar Herald, (FH)* 12 July 1907.
[12] Leneman, *A Guid Cause*, p. 258; FH 5 February 1909.
[13] Leneman, *A Guid Cause*, p. 77.
[14] Leneman, *A Guide Cause*, p. 258; FH 5 February 1909.
[15] FH 5 February 1909.

[16] FH, 21 September 1906; AG, 16 May 1906.
[17] Sanderson appears to have lived in a property in Castle Street, Forfar, with her husband who was actively involved with the local branch of the Independent Labour Party. FH 7 February 1908; FH, 6 March 1908.
[18] Leneman, *A Guid Cause*, p. 269.
[19] FH, 7 February 1908.
[20] FH, 7 February 1908.
[21] FH, 6 March 1908.
[22] FH, 6 March 1908.
[23] FH, 13 March 1908.
[24] FH, 13 March 1908.
[25] FH 16 May 1913; FH 12 September 1913.
[26] Arbroath Herald (AH), 8 October 1909.
[27] FH, 9 February 1912.
[28] E. King, 'The Scottish Women's Suffrage Movement' in E. Breitenbach and E. Gordon (eds), *Out of Bounds: Women in Scottish Society 1880-1945*, (Edinburgh, 1992), p. 139.
[29] AG, 9 May 1908.
[30] AG 16 May 1906; TS 4 October 1909.
[31] This organisation is listed in the *Arbroath and Eastern Angus Directory (AY)* and in 1939-40 two prominent members of the AWCA held the posts of Honorary President and Secretary and there were many more members in the committee of the YWCA indicating some sort of crossover.
[32] C. Beaumont, 'Citizens not Feminists: The Boundary Negotiated between Citizenship and Feminism by Mainstream Women's Organizations in England, 1928-1939', *Women's History Review*, Vol. 9, 2000, p. 416.
[33] Beaumont, *Citizens Not Feminists*, p. 416.
[34] AY 1891 p. 37; AY 1929-30 p. 62.
[35] AG, 6 December 1930.
[36] AY 1930-31, p. 62.

2

From Suffragists To Citizens

The period from 1918 onwards has been cited by many historians as much overlooked in relation to the history of the women's movement[1] and, according to Johanna Alberti, 'for the period which followed the war there are still only fragments' of that historical legacy left to posterity.[2] This neglect has had an obvious impact on the general populace as is highlighted by Dale Spender's genuine surprise to discover that 'there's always been a women's movement this century'.[3] This is because the campaigns that groups such as WCAs undertook are perceived not to have had the same excitement as those of the suffrage movement.[4] Indeed, the work of these groups has also suffered from an historical framework of inquiry that placed more emphasis on the work undertaken by individual women within conventional party politics and their election to political institutions, such as local government and parliament. In recent years, however, and with developments in gender theory, there has been a shift in historical interpretation in which there has been a move away from the old dichotomy of private versus public sphere that hitherto underpinned much historical study of the role and experience of women beyond the domestic sphere. This tendency overlooked the active and important role played by women involved in groups such as the WCA and therefore largely disregarded their contribution to political developments in Scotland – which explains their absence from the historical record and women's hidden history. It has now become more useful to think of political engagement in terms of spaces in which political exchange and engagement can occur beyond the public sphere and the remit of Parliament, municipal council authorities and political parties.[5] As Catriona Beaumont has noted, this widening of the historical agenda has revealed the need to examine why 'the role of middle-class, mainstream and non-political organisations for women in local and national affairs is still frequently underestimated and often ignored.'[6] This attempt to re-conceptualise the political has therefore opened up the way for historians to begin to analyse the political work of organisations such as the WCA.

This political work must be seen in its wider historical context, however, and it is clear that the inter-war period has been perceived as witnessing three main developments in the women's movement after securing equal voting rights in 1928. The first important development for the women's movement during this period was the emergence of a strong wave of anti-feminism. When war ended in 1918 many people hoped to be able to return to an era of peaceful relations. Indeed, Susan Kingsley Kent stresses that by attempting to create peace in the public sphere people 'imposed peace and order on the private sphere.'[7] Feminism was thus seen as a threat to the creation of this peaceful social order. Allied with this was the return of men from war looking to re-establish their dominant role in the public world. The wartime propaganda and the way in which the government had used women in this also contributed to what is believed to have been a gender backlash. Recruiting and propaganda posters with such slogans as 'Women of Britain Say 'Go!'' has led many historians to speculate that men viewed the horrors of war, and their participation in it, as somehow the fault of women.[8] Yet 1918 is identified as being a year of great advancement for women with all women over the age of thirty being granted the vote[9] - although this too helped produce a mild anti-feminist reaction.[10] It was clear, therefore, that there were many forces present in British society that were against any further political or legal gains for women, and that it would therefore take a strong and united women's movement to challenge the growth in anti-feminism.

The granting of the vote in 1918, however, did more to divide women than unite them. Indeed, it is believed that 'this victory was ... not followed by steady advance but by disagreements'.[11] The struggle for the vote clearly helped to unite a broad swathe of women, but exercising the right to vote only helped promote ever greater division. This division and the subsequent development of new feminism thus constitute a second important development influencing the women's movement. The suffragist groups of the pre-war years had varying success in the inter-war period. The militant WSPU emerged from the war as the Women's Party but had somewhat fizzled out by 1919.[12] The WFL carried on until 1961, but gradually became further isolated from the majority of women.[13] By far the most influential pre-war suffragist group to exert an influence in the years after 1918 was the NUWSS. In an attempt to incorporate the broad mass of women this society changed its name to the National Union of Societies for Equal Citizenship (NUSEC). A transition was therefore underway which would see the this group move from simply demanding the vote on equal terms as men, to become reformed into a campaign group with a much broader remit pushing for reforms that would enable women to become fully participating citizens in civil society.[14]

This change in direction for the women's movement was led by the NUSEC president Eleanor Rathbone. Her new brand of feminism was criticised by many who disagreed with the differences she highlighted between the genders and her emphasis on the role of mothers. Some of the equal-rights critics, such as Lady Rhondda, broke away and formed the Six Point Group in 1921. They agreed with Rathbone that the programme had to be broad, but they felt that clearer priorities had to be established.[15] Despite these divisions, however, these groups saw a degree of success and throughout the 1920s there was a raft of legislation introduced intended to improve the position of women in British society. According to Pat Thane 'at least sixteen pieces of legislation were introduced which were direct outcomes of organised campaigns by women's associations.'[16] Harold Smith, however, argues that most of this legislation actually only enhanced the status of mothers and thus the views of historians such as Thane 'overstates feminist responsibility for this legislation.'[17] It would appear, however, that the strength of anti-feminism was such that historians such as Smith may be too critical of new feminists and their welfare policies.

The criticisms of present-day historians, however, can also be seen in the inter-war period, and this led to a wider fragmentation of the women's movement. The theme of fragmentation, therefore, constitutes the third development to impact on the women's movement and this has been argued as being the 'chief characteristic of inter-war feminism'.[18] In 1927, some equal-rights members of the NUSEC resigned over the issue of campaigning for protective legislation, and this disagreement had its roots in the general discontent surrounding the direction Rathbone was taking the NUSEC.[19] In Rathbone's drive to incorporate the majority of women the NUSEC became divided into two organisations. The first of these was the National Council for Equal Citizenship that continued the work of a feminist pressure group. The second was known as the National Union of Townswomen's Guilds (TG). These were based on the popular Women's Institutes (WI) model and helped to promote the skills and interests of women as housewives.[20] They did, however, also participate in certain political campaigns such as increasing the number of policewomen and it was the TGs which became the dominant body within the NUSEC.[21] In giving such prominence to groups as the TGs the subject of other autonomous organisations who placed less emphasis on the skills of housewifery has been somewhat neglected. This may be the reason why some historians have come to the view that feminism, and more generally the women's movement, was in terminal decline by the 1930s.

It is clear that there was a flourishing associational culture for women during the interwar period and many new organisations were beginning to establish themselves during this time. One of the earliest was the Scottish Women's Rural Institutes, established in Longniddry in June 1917, which aimed to combat the isolation of countrywomen and to keep craftwork alive in rural communities.[22] Much later the Business and Professional Women's Federation (BPW) was established in 1938, and which aimed to 'awaken and encourage in business and professional women a realization of their responsibilities in their own country'.[23] Groups such as these all had in common a desire for 'doing things properly', which meant there were strict organisational procedures to adhere to in pursuing their goals and the manner in which they operated – while maintaining a keen sense of their past – and that they formed part of an international network of women. Furthermore, by training women so effectively in committee procedures they not only gave women a sense of comradeship but also gave them confidence and the opportunity to learn new skills that could set them up well for a role in local government if they so decided. They provided social outlets but at the same time they educated their members about their influence on society and how this could be put to good use.

The WCAs must be seen in the context of these autonomous women's organisations, yet their existence further indicates the general fragmentation within the women's movement at this time. Rathbone established the first WCA in Liverpool in 1913, some five years before women first gained the parliamentary vote. She believed that when the franchise was granted that there would be a need for a group to encourage and educate women on their new role in society.[24] The role of these WCAs was, therefore, to enable women to use their votes to better purpose through the study of public questions.[25] In 1917, a national council was set up under Mrs Ogilvie Gordon, and by 1918 branches were being formed across Britain.[26] A year later fifteen towns in Scotland had established WCAs and by then the Scottish Council (SCWCA) had also been established.[27] Two of the first WCAs established in Scotland were in Edinburgh and Dundee and both were inaugurated in 1918.[28]

Not only did these WCAs actively attempt to encourage women to enroll in their own associations, but they were also instrumental in the setting up of separate branches in other towns. An example of this is the establishment of the group in Forfar, the following notice for which appeared in the local press:

> [The] Honorary President of the Glasgow Women Citizens' Association invites the women of Forfar to meet … to form a local branch of the above Association.[29]

It is also apparent that the Honorary President of the DWCA, Lady Baxter, was to be present. This close co-operation between branches meant that by 1931 there were twenty WCAs in existence in Scotland alone.[30]

It is clear, therefore, that the women's movement in the period after the First World War underwent significant changes. The pressure from outside the women's movement, and, indeed, the divisions from within it, meant that by the end of the 1920s it lacked the cohesiveness of the suffrage campaign. Yet it would be unfair to suggest that all women's groups were more about domestic issues than about politics during this period as the agendas of the BPWs and the WCAs illustrate. Having gained equal voting rights by 1928, it was only to be expected that the movement would have to broaden out from the suffragist demand to claims for citizenship. Some of these national trends were also clearly reflected in local women's movements such as the one in Arbroath, where there was a clear shift from suffragist demands to claims of citizenship – as noted in the previous chapter. The other national development that is reflected here is the fragmentation of the movement. During the period 1930-45 there were many separate groups all vying for the attention of the female members of the Arbroath community, where we find an Arbroath Women's Cooperative Guild (WCG) and a Women's Section of the Labour Party, [31] and there was also an Arbroath Branch of the British Women's Temperance Society (one of the longest established and functioning women's organisations by the 1930s).[32] This is especially significant given Elspeth King's assertion that 'the political awareness of women was ... helped by the development of the temperance movement'.[33] Women's Rural Institutes also surrounded the town and there was even an Arbroath Ladies Guild of British Sailors.[34] This proliferation of women's groups highlights the national fragmentation of a movement that was once, to a greater or lesser extent, united behind the single issue of the vote.

It would appear, therefore, that some of the national developments taking place across Britain were reflected in Arbroath, but in particular the transition from suffrage to citizenship and the fragmentation of the women's movement. It is clearly the case that Arbroath had a thriving women's movement with many groups co-existing side-by-side and with each filling a different niche. This point is best exemplified by the fact that the 'Women's Health Enquiry' included Arbroath as one of its case studies. This investigated the health of 1,250 married working-class women and was published as *Working Class Wives* in 1939.[35] The 'Women's Health Enquiry' was made up from representatives of certain women's organisations. For Arbroath to be included in this enquiry was perhaps recognition of the fact that there was a particularly active and vocal women's movement operating there and that they were therefore in a good position to assist them in the conduct of their enquiry.[36] This enquiry also highlighted the need for health insurance for all women, that family allowance was essential and that there should be improved birth control advice for women.[37] Indeed, Martin Pugh argues that this enquiry 'serves as a reminder that new feminists were by no means as conservative as is sometimes suggested'.[38]

There was, therefore, much political activity undertaken by women nationally after the equal franchise was obtained and this activity was reflected to some extent in the activities of various women's groups at Arbroath. The women's movement was so well established at Arbroath that it obviously made conditions conducive not only for the Women's Health Enquiry to conduct its research there, but also ripe for the establishment of the Arbroath WCA. It is on this group that the remaining part of this book will concentrate.

NOTES

[1] For example, D. Beddoe, *Back to Home and Duty: Women Between the Wars 1918-1939*, (London, 1989), p. 132 and Caine, *English Feminism*, p. 172.

[2] J. Alberti, *Beyond Suffrage: Feminists in War and Peace*, 1914-1928, (London, 1989), p. 3.

[3] 'There's Always Been A Women's Movement this Century' is actually the title of Dale Spender's book (London, 1983). In this she attempts to highlight the myriad of different women's groups which existed in the inter-war period through the lives of five women.

[4] O. Banks, *The Politics of British Feminism 1918-1970*, (Aldershot, 1993), pp. 1-2.

[5] For this discussion see K. Hunt, 'Women as Citizens: Changing the Polity' in D. Simonton (ed), *The Routledge History of Women in Europe since 1700*, (Abingdon, 2006), pp. 216-220

[6] C. Beaumont, 'The Women's Movement, Politics and Citizenship 1918-1950s' in I. Zweiniger Bargielowska (ed), *Women in Twentieth Century Britain*, (Harlow, 2001), p. 275.

[7] S. Kingsley Kent, *Gender and Power in Britain, 1640-1990*, (London, 1999), pp. 294-5.

[8] For this viewpoint see Kingsley Kent, *Gender Reconstruction*, p. 69 and Caine, *English Feminism*, pp. 180-181.

[9] Although it is clear that the women who had done the majority of the war work

were not rewarded as the 1918 Act ensured that they remained voteless.

[10] Harrison, *Prudent Revolutionaries*, p. 1.
[11] Bryson, *Feminist Political Theory*, p. 99.
[12] Pugh, *Women's Movement*, p.45.
[13] Pugh, *Women's Movement*, p. 243.
[14] Banks, *Faces of Feminism*, p. 163.
[15] Caine, *English Feminism*, p. 184.
[16] P. Thane, 'Women's Participation in Political and Public Life: Building on Past Experience. What has changed and why since women got the vote?', *Women and Equality Unit*, December 2003, p. 2.
[17] H. L. Smith, 'British Feminism in the 1920s' in H. L. Smith, *British Feminism in the Twentieth Century*, (Aldershot, 1990), p. 52.
[18] Beddoe, *Back to Home and Duty*, p. 140.
[19] Banks, *Faces of Feminism*, pp. 170-1.
[20] Pugh, *Women's Movement*, pp. 240-1.
[21] Caine, *English Feminism*, p. 202.
[22] C. Blair, *Rural Journey – A History of the SWRI – From Cradle to Majority*, (Edinburgh, 1940), p. 72.
[23] D. V. Hall, *Making Things Happen: A History of the first 25 years of the Federation*, (London, 1963), p. 82.
[24] Pugh, *Women's Movement*, p. 50.
[25] Scottish Council of Women Citizens' Associations, *Handbook for Women Citizens Associations*, (Edinburgh, undated but c. 1968), p. 3.
[26] Caine, *English Feminism*, p. 201.
[27] SWCA, *Handbook*, p. 3.
[28] Innes, *Love and Work*, p. 157 and Watson, *Daughters of Dundee*, p. 201.
[29] FD, 10 January 1924.
[30] AG, 31 January 1931.
[31] AY, 1939-40, pp. 71-2.
[32] AY, 1939-40, p. 70.
[33] E. King, *The Scottish Women's Suffrage Movement*, (Glasgow, 1978), p. 10.
[34] AY, 1939-40, p. 75; p. 119.
[35] Pugh, *Women's Movement*, p. 250.
[36] M. Spring Rice, *Working Class Wives: Their Health and Conditions*, (London, 1979), p. 21.
[37] Pugh, *Women's Movement*, p. 251.
[38] Pugh, *Women's Movement*, p. 251.

3

Arbroath 'Women Citizens'

Objectives and Organisation

> *'Well, it took about 13 years for Arbroath*
> *to wake up to its women potential.'*[1]

This comment made by a former President of the AWCA highlights how long it took, in comparison to other places, to actually establish a WCA in Arbroath in 1931.[2] It would seem that the initiative for this came from the Dundee and Forfar branches, and the Presidents of both these groups, Mrs M. Mudie and Mrs Myles, were present at the inaugural meeting of the Arbroath branch. An advert appeared in the local press, as was the procedure for the establishment of these groups, inviting the women of Arbroath to attend and form a WCA.[3] At this meeting the aims and objectives of the association were set out and the principal speaker, Mrs Kemp Johnston of Dundee, declared that it was important for women to 'know about conducting business in a business-like manner'.[4] From the SCWCA minutes, however, it is clear that setting up a group in Arbroath was not a foregone conclusion, after the central organiser, who had been sent to encourage the formation of this group, reported that 'great difficulty was experienced in persuading anyone to take the responsibilities of office'.[5]

Despite such early drawbacks the first public meeting was held on 3 March 1931, with Lady Leslie MacKenzie, President of the SCWCA, the principal speaker. It was a well-attended meeting and in her speech she intimated that with women now having the vote it was important that they learnt all about what this implied and how they could take part in local and national government.[6] It was from this platform that the Arbroath 'women citizens' built their association[7] and the aims of WCAs simply set out:

1. To foster a sense of citizenship in women

2. To encourage self-education in political, civic and economic questions

3. To secure an adequate representation of the interests and experiences of women in the affairs of the community.[8]

The idea of citizenship was a popular one for most female organisations during this period, and according to Catriona Beaumont they opted for 'the rhetoric of citizenship and citizenship rights' in order to campaign for reforms beneficial to women and crucially to retain their popularity.[9] Citizenship for these groups, however, appeared to mean more about emphasising women's new rights and more importantly was an overarching concept which it was hoped would overcome issues of religion and class.[10]

Similar to other WCA branches the Arbroath group divided its work into separate committees. During the period 1931-45 this included work on the infirmary, cinemas, housing, mental deficiency, vagrancy, probation and maternity.[11] It is evident that the interests of this association were varied and that they had concerns about a wide range of social issues. They held a number of different meetings during a session (annual period of operation) including on average five public meetings that brought a speaker of interest to talk on a certain topic to which anyone could attend. There were also six member meetings each session, including an Annual General Meeting, which took the form of talks, and other social events such as Supper Parties. At each AGM the committee for the following session was elected. This committee then met exclusively from the association to talk about any administrative issues that may have arisen. The key concept for all work was that of organisation and a need to train women effectively in committee procedures. Any nomination for the committee or any resolution to be passed had to be seconded by another member and formally passed through the chair. 'Women Citizens' had a keen sense of doing things right and sticking rigidly to procedure. Their method of continuous meetings and lobbying of influential people has led some historians, including Barbara Caine, to conclude that this quieter way of doing things 'made their work less visible'.[12] This invisibility seriously overlooks the vibrancy of these groups and the important political forums they constituted.

The AWCA was also affiliated to the broader Scottish Council which was established in 1919, and from this body four area committees were established. The AWCA was in North-East division along with Dundee, Forfar, Brechin, St Andrews, Broughty Ferry and Tayport, and each year a North-East conference was organised with each town in turn hosting the event. These events were seen as key in enabling women to discuss important legislative measures on a non-party basis, and that women should take steps to adjust their status so as to enable them to make their fullest contribution to national welfare.[13]

This idea of welfare was central to the work of the AWCA. This function saw them attract some criticism and led to accusations that they concentrated too much on welfare issues and in doing so were neglecting the needs of women in paid work and the improvement of women in public life. It has been argued that this 'welfare' or 'new' feminism forgot the feminist purpose behind the welfare goals, and Susan Kingsley Kent suggests that their ideological approach became confused with that of anti-feminists.[14] In contrast, Seth Koven and Sonya Michel have argued that these welfare feminists actually challenged the boundaries between the private and the public, believing that they 'transformed motherhood from women's primary private responsibility into public policy'.[15] It would, therefore, appear that some of the criticisms with regards to the WCAs' focus on welfare reform are in the main unfair, and that the women involved played a crucial role in advancing the position of women and contributing to British society more generally. It is rather short-sighted in any case to assert that the WCAs were mainly concerned with welfare issues. They were also concerned with issues of equality and therefore the distinctions between welfare and equality are not always clearly cut and dried within a group of this nature. They continually blurred the line drawn between competing gender and feminist theories. Indeed, it is evident that the AWCA was successful in combining different theories and that by doing so they were able to highlight and identify a vast array of problems that were of concern to the women's movement at this time.

The Membership

Their ability to attract many from the upper class of Arbroath society helped to legitimise the cause of the AWCA. There was a small core of women who were influential in the establishment and the subsequent running of the Arbroath WCA. The most influential founder member among this group was Mrs Corsar, wife of ex-Bailie Harry Corsar (who was married into one of the oldest textile families of Arbroath).[16] She presided over the inaugural meeting of the AWCA and was also influential in the Red Cross Society, the Girl Guides and was the Secretary of the Female Home Mission.[17] Her untimely death in March 1931, cut short her presidency of the AWCA after only a few months and shocked the community of Arbroath. In her obituary she was described as a 'prominent woman citizen' and it was noted that 'few ladies in Arbroath [were] better known [or] held in higher esteem'.[18] It was clear that she had been a much respected citizen of Arbroath and that her philanthropic and voluntary work had earned her much credit. Whilst not presiding over the AWCA for long she was highly influential in having helped to establish it and quite probably was instrumental in initially attracting other women to the group. Her commitment to the creation of this association indicated how important it was that active and influential members of the community attached themselves to the cause of the WCAs.

The main driving force in the AWCA thereafter, however, was Miss Ann Hampton (who has proved very problematic to research as very little is known of her today). She was a member of the AWCA from its inception right up until the 1960s, and was President during 1933 to 1934, and in 1935 was conferred the title of Honorary President.[19] She was also nominated for the Presidency of the SCWCA, an honour that highlights how well respected she was not only in Arbroath but by the WCA movement as a whole.[20] Indeed, it is unclear why many people have never heard of Ann Hampton; the only information being obtained from her gravestone and her obituaries in the *Arbroath Herald* and *Arbroath Guide*. From this it is evident that she was educated at Arbroath High School, Harris Academy and University College, Dundee where she gained the qualification of L.L.A. Hons[21] (L.L.A. signifies Lady Literate in Arts, which was on offer at St Andrews University from 1877)[22], and perhaps more significantly she also studied abroad at the Sorbonne. Thereafter she set out on a teaching career at Kinghorn High School, Perth, first becoming the head of modern languages and then headmistress of Cockburn High School in Leeds.[23] This would indicate that she was a lady of some intelligence who believed that education could be used to greater purpose. It is also indicative that she was part of a quite progressive family of whom her father, Peter, was the local veterinary surgeon.[24]

Ann Hampton returned to Arbroath in the 1930s after she retired and immediately became immersed in public affairs in Arbroath. Among other things she was honorary secretary of the Arbroath Ladies' Guild of British Sailors Society for twenty-one years and was also a member of the Ladies Lifeboat Guild. She died in 1962 at the age of eighty-eight. The local paper reported that 'Well-Known Arbroath Lady' Miss Ann Hampton had died, and it was clearly a matter of importance to the local community.[25] More column inches were dedicated to Ann than to her younger sister upon her death even though Ann had lived more years away from Arbroath. This arguably highlights the impact she made working in the voluntary sector and on the community of Arbroath.

Ann Hampton also had two younger siblings: her brother Peter and sister Helen Airth. Helen joined the AWCA some time after Ann and she actively contributed to many of their campaigns bringing much enthusiasm to these activities. She followed an identical educational path to that of her sister and obviously keen to extend her education, studied biology and science in the Yorkshire College, and began teaching at Cockburn High School, Leeds in 1896. Helen returned to Arbroath in 1898 - much earlier than Ann – where she took up the post of infant mistress of Ladyloan School, then

Parkhouse School, Abbey School and finally Inverbrothock School.[26] Her and Ann's importance is that they were professional women in their own right, both being teachers. This meant that the AWCA had a mix of women like Ann and Helen and others who were recognised as being married to influential men.

Two women who were married to influential men and who did make names for themselves in Arbroath were Mrs McCrae Wilson and Mrs Matthew. Mrs McCrae Wilson married a businessman and owner of a prominent furniture outlet, D. P. Wilson and Sons, while Mrs Matthew was married to the owner of a local tailoring firm Matthew and Son.[27] This meant that they mixed with the prominent business classes of Arbroath, but the AWCA gave them the platform to move beyond this. Mrs Matthew appears to have been a member of the AWCA committee from 1931, with Mrs McCrae Wilson joining three years later. Both became presidents during the 1930s and presided over such committees as Housing and the Cinema. Indeed, Mrs Matthew was given the additional title of Honorary President during the 1950s and received a further honour from the community when she became Bailie of Arbroath.[28] There are many examples of the invaluable work that both Mrs McCrae Wilson and Mrs Matthew did on behalf of the community of Arbroath and for women more generally during their time in the AWCA. For example, Mrs McCrae Wilson was chosen to sit on the Local National Service Committee as the representative of the AWCA, and both were selected as town councillors in 1942.[29] The function and operation of the AWCA and the manner in which they structured meetings and committees was an ideal preparation for their later participation in local government and other non-governmental bodies. It is quite clear, therefore, that Martin Pugh is correct to assert that the WCAs were 'largely middle-class and non-party in character'.[30] Other historians have come to similar conclusions. Sue Innes noted that the Edinburgh WCA 'was a formal, liberal feminist and middle-class organisation', and likewise Norman Watson stressed that the members of the Dundee WCA 'were largely middle-class'.[31]

It is apparent that the members of the executive committee of the AWCA all lived in a middle-class area of Arbroath, predominantly situated in the Keptie and Lochlands ward area, and most lived in close proximity to each other.[32] Clearly, the AWCA was middle-class in outlook and orientation, but did this prohibit them from associating with working class organisations? Innes found no evidence linking the Edinburgh WCA and the women in the labour movement.[33] There is evidence that demonstrates that the AWCA had links with the labour movement and this was apparent in the early 1940s when various women's groups rallied in support of the establishment of a maternity house at Arbroath. From the minutes of the AWCA it is clear that the local Women's Co-operative Guild and the Women's Labour Party had sent letters to the Town Council stating the need for such a facility, and in supporting this initiative the AWCA proposed that:

> ... a letter be sent to each of these parties
> thanking them for bringing up the matter
> and to say the Women Citizens'
> Association would be glad to co-operate.[34]

This clearly indicates a close co-operation between what was a mainly middle-class organisation and other groups that represented working class women and the labour movement, but it would appear that the AWCA did have a working-class membership. At the inaugural meeting of this association the local newspapers reported a 'large and representative attendance' and this could indicate that whilst middle-class women held the top positions in this group that there was indeed some working-class women among the membership.[35] Indeed, it would appear that the AWCA was significantly different in its make-up from other WCAs. Other WCAs usually attracted titled members, for example Lady Baxter led the DWCA and the Forfar WCA (FWCA) had the Countess of Strathmore as their Honorary President,[36] and Innes noted that within the EWCA there was 'a smattering of titles' including Lady Leslie MacKenzie.[37] Within the ranks of the AWCA, however, there was no sign of any aristocratic members and this was perhaps why they had more substantial links with the labour movement than some other WCAs.

Membership of the AWCA, like all WCAs, was open to all women over eighteen and a minimum annual subscription was charged in order to defray expenses, and it is clear that the AWCA was successful in attracting a large membership. For example, during its first session 1931-32, it attracted 124 women and by 1938, this had increased to 205 members. Table I indicates the general increase in these numbers and although this declines out somewhat with the onset of World War Two, membership remains fairly high thereafter.

Table I: Membership Number of the AWCA 1931-1945

Session	Number of Members
1931-1932	124
1932-1933	134
1933-1934	139
1934-1935*	--
1935-1936*	--
1936-1937	177
1937-1938	204
1938-1939	205
1939-1940	165
1940-1941	181
1941-1942	175
1942-1943*	--
1943-1944	174
1944-1945	176

(Source: Annual Reports in the AWCA Minute Books 1931-1945)
Numbers for these sessions are not available

These numbers are in fact fairly high when compared to English WCAs which at this time had an average of between sixty and eighty members.[38] This was not peculiar to Arbroath as all WCAs in the North East of Scotland had high membership. For example, the Dundee branch had a membership of around one thousand women.[39]

What is significant, however, is in comparison with Dundee, Arbroath had a higher proportion of 'women citizens' in relation to population numbers, as highlighted in Table II.

Table II: Proportion of 'Women Citizens' in Relation to Population in Arbroath and Dundee

	Optimum Membership	Size of Population (1931)	Proportion of Members in Relation to Population (%)*
Arbroath	205	17,653	1.2
Dundee	1000	177,000	0.6

(Source: figures taken from Watson's *'Daughters of Dundee'* and for Arbroath the minute books of the AWCA and the Arbroath Directory).
Figures rounded up to one decimal point

The AWCA had popular support and was widely accepted by the community. Prominent members of local government came to speak to the group, such as the Public Assistance Officer and the local M.P. Indeed, Provost Chapel frequently attended the meetings of the AWCA and on such occasions was usually accompanied by his wife. This is a clear indication that the AWCA were regarded as an important political forum and one which local politicians thought it necessary to address. The effectiveness of the Arbroath branch, however, was based on the simple fact that they attracted high numbers of women to the cause, and this made the organisation an important part of the local community.

NOTES

[1]   C. H. Florence, *The History of the Scottish Women's Association and the Arbroath Women's Association 1931-2003*, (Unpublished manuscript, 2003), p. 1.

2   Both Edinburgh and Dundee were established in 1918 and the *Forfar Directory* states that the FWCA began in 1924 (p. 83).

3   AG, 31 January 1931.

4   AG, 7 February 1931.

5   SCWCA Minute Book 1919-1932, 30 January 1931.

6   AG 7 March 1931.

7   This was how they were commonly referred to in newspapers and how they frequently referred to themselves in their minutes.

8   AWCA Syllabus Card 1938-9.

9   Beaumont, *Citizens not Feminists*, p. 416.

10   For this view see Innes, *Love and Work*, p. 162.

11   Various references to these committees can be found in the AWCA minute books 1931-45.

12   Caine, *English Feminism*, p. 173.

13   SCWCA, Handbook, pp. 2-8.

14   Banks, *Faces of Feminism*, p. 177 and Kingsley Kent, *Gender and Power*, p. 302.

15   S. Koven and S. Michel in H. Jones, *Women in British Public Life 1914-1950: Gender, Power and Social Policy*, (Harlow, 2000), p. 4 and pp. 73-4.

16   AY, 1932-33, p. 10 and W.H.K. Turner, *The Textile Industry of Arbroath since the early 18th century*, (Dundee, 1954), p. 26.

17   AG 14 March 1931.

18   AY, 1932-3, p. 10; AG 14 March 1931.

19   Information obtained from the AWCA Syllabus Cards which are held with the minute books and detail activities for each session.

20   AWCA Minute Book, 13 December 1934.

21   AH, February 23 1962.

22   Leneman, *Guid Cause*, p. 15.

23   AH February 23 1962.

24   AG February 24 1962.

25   AH February 23 1962.

26   AH February 14 1969.

27   Information obtained from the Arbroath yearbooks and adverts from the local newspapers.

28   Information obtained from AWCA Syllabus cards 1950-5.

29   AWCA Minute Book, Annual Report 1942-1943.

30   Pugh, *Women's Movement*, p. 51.

31   Innes, *Love and Work*, p. 160; Watson, *Daughters of Dundee*, p. 220.

32   Addresses obtained from AWCA Minute Books.

33   Innes, *Love and Work*, p. 155.

34   AWCA Minute Book 19 January 1943.

35   AG 7 February 1931.

36   The Forfar Directory, 1935, p. 82.

37   Innes, *Love and Work*, p. 160.

38   Watson, *Daughters of Dundee*, p. 216.

39   Watson, *Daughters of Dundee*, p. 216.

Plate 1:
Suffragettes in Forfar:
Flora Drummond is seated nearest the front in the back of the car.

Plate 2:
Flora Drummond: Working in the WSPU offices in London.

Plate 3:
Suffragette Caravan, 1913: Helen Fraser (on the far right), in woods in Angus, helping to set up a caravan which she toured Scotland in.

Plate 4:
Mrs Amy Sanderson, 1910.

Plate 5:
Suffragettes at Brothock Bridge, Arbroath, 1911.

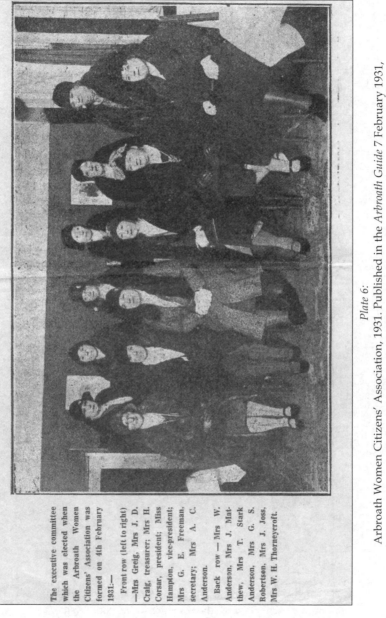

The executive committee which was elected when the Arbroath Women Citizens' Association was formed on 4th February 1931:—

Front row (left to right) —Mrs Greig, Mrs J. D. Craig, treasurer; Mrs H. Corsar, president; Miss Hampton, vice-president; Mrs G. E. Freeman, secretary; Mrs A. C. Anderson.

Back row — Mrs W. Anderson, Mrs J. Matthew, Mrs T. Stark Anderson, Mrs G. S. Robertson, Mrs J. Joss, Mrs W. H. Thorneycroft.

Plate 6:
Arbroath Women Citizens' Association, 1931. Published in the *Arbroath Guide* 7 February 1931, pictured here are the founder members of the association.

Women Citizens' Association

(ARBROATH BRANCH)

Session 1937-1938.

Hon. Presidents :
Mrs HARLEY, Brigton.
Miss HAMPTON, Rosedene.

President :
Mrs JOHN PATTERSON, 19 Viewfield Road.

Vice-Presidents :
Mrs A. McCRAE WILSON, Woodlands.
Mrs MATTHEW, Crandart.

Secretary :
Mrs WILKIE, Clivedene, Viewfield Road.

Joint Treasurers :
Mrs GARVIE, Commercial Bank House.
Mrs FERRIER, 6 Montrose Road.

Convener of Entertainment Committee :
Mrs BENNETT.

T. BUNCLE AND CO. LTD.

AIMS OF THE ASSOCIATION.

1. To foster a sense of citizenship in women.

2. To encourage self-education in political, civic and economic questions.

3. To secure an adequate representation of the interests and experience of women in the affairs of the community.

MEMBERSHIP.

All women over 18 are eligible for membership. The minimum annual subscription is 1/-, payable at the beginning of the session.

SYLLABUS.

PUBLIC MEETINGS.

1937.
Oct. 5—" Through the Central Highlands by Wade's Roads " (Illustrated by Lantern Slides).
J. B. SALMOND, Esq., Dundee.

Nov. 2—" Nursery Schools."
Miss EDITH LUKE, M.B.E., M.A., Dundee.

Dec. 7—" Scottish National Mark Products."
Cinema Lecture by a Marketing Officer of the Department of Agriculture.

1938.
Feb. 1—" The Cinema : Censorship and Control."
Miss M. I. ADAM, Greenock.

Mar. 1—" Dietetics."
Miss MARY ANDROSS, B.Sc., Glasgow.

PUBLIC MEETINGS are held in the Assembly Hall, at 7.30 p.m. prompt.

MEETINGS FOR MEMBERS.

1937.
Oct. 19—Members' Social Evening in Soutar's Rooms.
Whist. Dancing.

Nov. 16—Short Talks by Members.
Demonstration of Weaving and other Handicrafts by Miss NETTIE LAMB, Brechin.

1938.
Jan. 18—" The Romance of our Countryside."
Lecture Recital by Mrs HUTTON, Perth.

Feb. 15—" Chairs and their History."
ALAN INGLIS, Esq., F.S.A.(Scot.).

Mar. 15—Supper Party.

Mar. 29—General Business Meeting. Group Discussions.

MEETINGS FOR MEMBERS are held in Soutar's Rooms, at 7.30 p.m. prompt.

COUNTRY DANCING CLASS, conducted by Mrs G. S. Robertson, resumes Monday, 11th October, in the Wesleyan Hall.

Plate 7:
Front and Inside of Arbroath Women Citizens' Association Syllabus Card 1937-38. This session covered a varied selection of talks including on 'nursery schools' and 'the romance of the countryside.'

Plate 8:
Front cover of the Scottish Council of Women Citizens' Association Handbook.

WOMEN CITIZENS' CONFERENCE IN NORTH SEA HOTEL.

Front (left to right)—Mrs John Matthew, Miss M'Intosh, Forfar; Miss Hampton (President, Arbroath branch), Mrs Allardice, Forfar; Miss Millar, Tayport.

Plate 9:
Women Citizens' Association North East Area Conference.
This first appeared in the *Arbroath Herald* 9 February 1934, and includes members from Forfar, Tayport and host town, Arbroath.

Plate 10:
Arbroath Women Citizens' Association Work Party.
This group concentrated on making items from wool for the war effort.
This picture was taken from the *Arbroath Guide*, 11 September 1941.

4

'Filling a Need': AWCA Work 1931-1945

Most accounts that chart the developments of the women's movement after the granting of equal franchise focus on its decline. For example, Deirdre Beddoe has argued that 'it was in the 1930s that the movement really began to dwindle'.[1] More recently historians have sought to revise this view. Sue Innes rejected the notion of a decline in activity and argued instead that the women's movement witnessed 'increased participation by women in public and political life'.[2] The evidence presented thus far in this study would clearly support the revisionist view, and in order to further press this case this chapter will look at the campaigns conducted by the AWCA during the period 1931 to 1945 and assess how successful these were. It will be demonstrated that the revisionists are indeed correct in highlighting and correcting the popular misconception that after 1928 the women's movement fell into inexorable decline.

1931-1934: The Formative Years
The period of 1931 to 1934 was a rather quiet one for initiating reforms as the AWCA set about attempting to establish themselves within the wider community. One of the first objectives that they set themselves, however, was to get a woman placed on the Arbroath Infirmary Committee.[3] This was a clear indication of their support for welfare reform at a local level, although their efforts in this case ended in failure. There is no evidence of them managing to co-opt any member onto this committee, but the membership still had an involvement and was involved in fund-raising – a Mrs Harley, for example, organised a garden fete for the benefit of the Infirmary.[4] At this juncture, however, it would appear that it was acceptable for the AWCA to raise funds for local bodies but not to participate in the decision-making process. Norman Watson has also found evidence

of reluctance on the part of the Dundee Royal Infirmary board to co-opt members of the DWCA, although some members were admitted onto the committee in 1922.[5] It is evident that where some issues were concerned, the process of change would be slow. It would seem that while prominent men often encouraged women in their welfare work when this appeared to challenge the status quo, and more specifically government and local authority policies that underlined and maintained male authority, such public figures became more reticent.[6]

A second objective that the members of the AWCA set themselves in this formative period was the revision of the Indian Women's Franchise. During the early 1930s many British feminists were championing the rights of Indian women. Eleanor Rathbone, after touring India for six weeks, spearheaded this campaign.[7] In supporting this campaign, Innes noted, it is clear that equality issues came to be viewed as 'an important part of their work'.[8] Indeed, during one particular meeting the AWCA passed a resolution to urge that the voting strength of Indian women should not be less than one woman to four-and-a-half men. The secretary was then instructed to write to the Chairman of the Select Committee for Indian Constitutional Reform.[9] Nationally, this campaign was successful in helping to widen the concessions to female voters in India, but it failed to gain assurances for their civil rights.[10] This objective, however, is useful in highlighting how the AWCA incorporated both elements of welfare and equal-rights feminism in their work. It can also be seen that they were co-operating with a campaign that had national implications and that their interests stretched beyond the confines of the community of Arbroath.

A further objective that had national implications related to the AWCAs involvement in the aforementioned 'Women's Health Enquiry'. This was set up to investigate the lives of working-class women and offer some suggestions as to how their lives could be improved. A letter was sent to the AWCA and as a group, it was decided not to take the matter any further. It was noted, however, that 'several members thought they might be able to do something and it was agreed that they might do so as individuals'.[11] Clearly, this issue was important to some within the ranks of the AWCA.

The issues that generally interested the AWCA can be gauged by perusing their lecture syllabus. One such lecture considered 'Recent Discoveries in Medicine and their Application to Public Health'. When this lecture ended, however, it was followed by a demonstration of the latest vacuum cleaner. This indicates quite explicitly the varied interests of the AWCA, that pointed to an active interest in political and welfare issues on the one hand, and a clear example of domesticity on the other.[12] Indeed, it was during the 1930s that the domestic ideal became more attainable through the production of such things as vacuum cleaners and other such labour-saving devices.[13]   In contrast, in a lecture presented by Dr W. J. Dewar, the membership of the AWCA was pressed to put forward candidates at the forthcoming municipal elections for election to the Town Council.[14]   It would appear that there were some men in Arbroath who supported the advancement of women into roles in public life. There was also a lecture on 'Careers for Girls' where the AWCA were told of the expanding opportunities for women in the civil service, and how 'women proved as capable of filling the big posts of the scholastic profession as men'.[15] This gives a clear indication that the AWCA did not concentrate solely on issues surrounding women in the home, but were also interested in discussing aspects of women's employment.

It is evident, however, that in terms of meeting their stated objectives the AWCA did not meet with much success in the period 1931 to 1934. They were, however, building a strong base from which to establish themselves and help implement future reforms. The association was, however, still thriving and even at this point it would be rather short-sighted to suggest that the women's movement was in decline in the 1930s.

1935-1938: 'Filling a Need'[16]

During the period 1935 to 1939 the AWCA concentrated more fully on the welfare needs of women as wives and mothers and were thus adhering more firmly to the new feminist ideology. The AWCA's work was focused mainly on the setting up of an endowment fund for the sole purpose of buying a bed for the maternity wing in the Local Infirmary.[17] Ann Hampton was the driving force behind this and in turn headed up the committee that was established to raise funds.[18] Many inter-war women's organisations concentrated on welfare issues and thus the AWCA must be seen as quite typical of this development. Pat Thane argued that they 'did prioritise welfare with good reason' as the depression and its consequences had focused attention on the poor living standards of working-class wives and mothers.[19] Indeed, in many respects middle-class women took up the issue of welfare in the 1930s from the labour movement in the same manner as they had done prior to World War One.[20] The concern of new feminists was 'to secure some real improvement in the welfare of wives and mothers', but as Jane Lewis argued this 'by no means implied a rejection of the equal rights philosophy'.[21] Indeed, by doing this it can be seen that they were moving away from defining equality for women on purely masculine terms.

A further example of the concern surrounding welfare issues was presented in a lecture to the AWCA, by Dr Agnes Thomson, on the subject of 'Maternity and Child Welfare Services'.[22] Thomson stated that there was a grave need for establishing social services that were aimed at promoting health and preventing disease, and that her main aim was to reduce the mortality among infants and mothers. This in turn would save 'many lives whose brains, energy and intelligence might one day be of the greatest possible value to the nation'.[23]

The AWCA, during the period 1935 to 1938, were also concerned with the issue of nursery schools. Miss Edith Luke, Mistress of Method at Dundee Training College, lectured to them on this topic, and stressed how the Education Act of 1918 had given powers to education authorities to establish nursery schools, but that most of them still had to be maintained by voluntary subscription.[24] It is evident, therefore, that women at this time had a substantial influence in shaping welfare policies by promoting a 'maternalist' political agenda and that this was chiefly though the pressure exerted by voluntary groups.[25] As Luke suggested, maternalism highlighted how investment in children now would 'be balanced by the money saved later on hospitals, reformatories and prisons'.[26] There was a long waiting list for the nursery school in Dundee and this indicated the pressing need for childcare facilities to help mothers in employment.[27] This subject shows the adherence of the AWCA to both new and equal-rights feminism in so far as they championed the cause of child welfare while also promoting an issue which enabled women to work. The period of 1935 to 1938 can be seen to have concentrated on welfare policies in strict adherence to the new feminist philosophy, but there was also the early indication that equal rights issues were becoming more important and would come to the fore in later work.

1939-1945: War Work

The adherence of the AWCA to new feminist ideology continued on into the period 1939 to 1945, and a clear example of this was their continued commitment to funding the infirmary. Indeed, they handed over £100 to the Infirmary Centenary Fund for the sole purpose of buying a bed for the Maternity Home (indeed, enquiries were then made by the group to ascertain the possibility of naming the bed once the new home was established).[28] This activity illustrates very effectively that new feminists concentrated on the needs of women as mothers rather than the rights of women.[29] It is clear, however, that the AWCA did not solely concentrate on women as mothers, and that the period of World War Two created a more liberal environment which encouraged the AWCA to embrace the campaign for equal rights as the AWCA threw themselves into all manner of wartime work. Indeed, Thane argues that 'World War Two in the short run provided wider career opportunities and openings in public life for women, due to the absence of men'.[30] It is also clear that the Government were more willing to co-opt women onto committees during this period with members of the AWCA represented on the local committees for National Service, the Ministry of Labour and the Ministry of Information.[31] The AWCA also divided themselves into work parties during this period. The activities undertaken by the Arbroath 'Women Citizens' ranged from organising National Savings Stamps, to knitting articles and distributing wool in order to raise money for the armed forces.[32] There was quite a response to this work, for example during the session 1939 to 1940 some 200 articles were knitted and a further 100 sewn.[33] The work done by the AWCA at this time clearly supports Sue Bruley's argument that 'there is no doubt that women volunteers were the backbone of the war effort on the home front.'[34]

Nationally the effort on the home front was organised by the Women's Voluntary Services (WVS). This was set up by the Home Office in 1938 and headed by Lady Reading. Its growth was phenomenal and by the end of the war half-a-million women were involved in WVS activities.[35] As a branch, the AWCA could not undertake this kind of work but it was resolved that individuals could do so, and Mrs Patterson, the then President, 'urged all those on the committee who had not enrolled to do so'.[36] This began a long partnership between the AWCA and WVS and together they also established a nursery school and a social centre for evacuated mothers and children: the social centre in particular was considered to be 'very successful'.[37]

The AWCA also contributed to 'Aid to Russia Fund' – another national campaign – and a whist drive organised to raise funds amassed a healthy sum of £21.12.6.[38] Clementine Churchill headed this particular campaign, which Jones asserted 'caught the public's imagination and aroused far more sympathy and support than any other aid to allies'.[39] The success of this campaign is not in doubt for by the end of the war over £7 million had been raised nationally.[40] War work also enabled the AWCA to become more deeply involved in the equal-rights campaigns and it is clear too that 'the war brought with it something of a renewed interest in feminist issues'.[41]

One example of the increasing public role of women was the growing numbers present in the police force during this period. This was initiated by Miss Ann Hampton who sent a resolution to the SCWCA as early as 1941 stating that there should be 'a police woman in every garrison town'.[42] The campaign nationally clearly had an impact for in 1939 there were only 174 policewomen out of a total force of 65,000, at its peak, by June 1943, there were over 7,300 women serving in the police.[43] There were two distinct groups of women police that emerged during the war: the Women Police Service and Women Patrols.[44] These laid the foundations for the later development of women police and the AWCA can be viewed as making a positive contribution to this campaign. In February 1943, Miss Hampton proposed a resolution be sent to the Women's Council meeting in Glasgow to the effect that 'this association desires to express the urgent need for more police women in Scotland' and this was then seconded by the FWCA.[45] This campaign then gained momentum with a letter being sent to the Town Council via the Town Clerk pointing out that there was a need for women police in Scottish towns.[46] Reference to this letter is made in the Town Council minute books where it was noted:

> 'There was submitted a letter, dated 18th May, from the Arbroath Women Citizens' Association regarding the appointment of Policewomen. The Chief Constable submitted a report stating that he did not consider the appointment of Policewomen was required in the Burgh, and the Town Clerk was instructed to inform the Association accordingly.'[47]

It is quite apparent, therefore, why Jane Lewis argued that any gains for women would be 'achieved in the face of male resistance'.[48] The AWCA did have some success, however, in getting this issue adopted by the SCWCA as it is clear that they made representations to the Local Authorities on this subject and helped encourage the police force to recruit more women.[49] Indeed, the appointment of policewomen was something that became a continuing campaigning issue for the SCWCA.[50]

A further equality issue that the AWCA considered during this period was that of pay, and two lectures presented in the session 1944 to 1945 brought this subject to prominence. The first was given by Mrs Matthew on the issue of 'Equal and Unequal Pay', and the second was entitled 'Tomorrow's Women' presented by Mrs S. R. Irvine of the FWCA.[51] The talk by Mrs Irvine considered women in employment, within the home and in public life. This is a clear indication that WCAs did not simply consider women as wives and mothers, but as individuals partaking in a myriad of other activities. Thane highlights this point by stating that inter-war feminists have been criticised for focusing too narrowly on welfare issues when in reality they were also concerned with women in employment and the issue of equal pay.[52]

The ultimate success for the AWCA during this time was the appointment of two of their members as Town Councillors, and in the Annual Report of 1942 to 1943 it was noted with some pride that:

> … our Association has been honoured by
> two of our past Presidents having become
> Town Councillors namely Mrs J. Matthew
> and Mrs McCrae Wilson. They have our
> heartiest congratulations.'[53]

Bruley argued that at a local level women were able to make more of an impact and that 'many aspiring women politicians gained their political spurs in local government'.[54] This would seem to be the case in Arbroath where the town council minutes suggest that the AWCA members received a warm welcome and in relation to Mrs McCrae Wilson's appointment that 'Provost Sir William Chapel extended to her a cordial welcome as a member of the Town Council.'[55] During their time they served on many committees and Mrs Matthew became convener of the Public Health Hospital.[56]

By becoming Councillors these two women were then able to educate the AWCA on the workings of local government. Mrs Matthew addressed the AWCA on 'Present Day Topics' submitting a sketch of the Town Council Chambers and explaining the duties that each member had to undertake. Mrs McCrae Wilson also talked during this address on the subject of post-war development stating that she desired to see 'mothers take their proper place in the social circle, and not confine themselves entirely to domesticity'.[57] This is a clear indication that whilst the AWCA adhered predominantly to new feminism, they also believed in equal rights issues and had made the move into local politics. This confirms Pugh's assertion that 'local government clearly provided an attractive field of endeavour' for many members of the women's movement.[58]

The period 1939 to 1945, therefore, opened up new possibilities for women of the AWCA. The government looked to women to keep the home front going and in doing so enabled them to partake in activities which had previously been thought only as the preserve of men. The AWCA capitalised on this to raise issues of equality such as the need for women police and equal pay and in doing so propelled themselves into local politics. In contrast to the First World War, therefore, which interrupted the women's movement at its peak, the Second World War appeared to create something of a revival.[59]

Thus it is evident that the women's movement was very much alive and active in Arbroath during the 1930s and beyond, providing a clear example that the granting of equal franchise in 1928 did not bring to an end these activities. Historians also tend to focus on the welfare activities of the NUSEC and as a result have paid insufficient attention to the workings of such groups as the AWCA who were promoting equal rights issues within their community.[60] This neglect has, therefore, led to a misconception that the year 1928 witnessed a decline in female political campaigning, for clearly, and as the evidence produced in this study thus far suggests, the arguments of revisionist historians have shown that this view is no longer tenable.

NOTES

[1]   Beddoe, *Back to Home and Duty*, p. 140.
[2]   S. Innes, Constructing Women's Citizenship in the Interwar Period: the Edinburgh Women Citizens' Association, *Women's History Review*, Vol. 13, November 2004, p. 621.
[3]   AWCA Minute Book, 21 May 1931.
[4]   Arbroath Infirmary Minute Books, 27 May 1931, p. 23.
[5]   Watson, *Daughters of Dundee*, p. 210.
[6]   Koven and Michel in Jones, *British Public Life*, p. 5.
[7]   Harrison, *Prudent Revolutionaries*, p. 113.
[8]   Innes, *Love and Work*, p. 210.
[9]   AWCA Minute Book, 10 June 1933.
[10] Harrison, *Prudent Revolutionaries*, p. 113.
[11] AWCA Minute Book, 11 September 1934.
[12] AWCA Minute Book, 24 November 1931
[13] M. Pugh, 'Domesticity and the Decline of Feminism, 1930-1950' in H. L. Smith, *British Feminism in the Twentieth Century*, (Aldershot, 1990), pp. 152-3.
[14] AH, 5 October 1934
[15] AH 7 December 1934
[16] This comes from an article in the AH, 9 October 1934: 'the association was entering its seventh year and annually increasing membership encouraged the belief that they were filling a need in the lives of the women of the town.'

17 AWCA Minute Book, 6 April 1937.
18 AWCA Minute Book, 26 January 1937.
19 Thane, *Women's Participation*, p. 4.
20 J. Lewis, 'Feminism and Welfare' in J. Mitchell and A. Oakley (eds), *What is Feminism?*, (Oxford, 1986), p. 92.
21 Lewis, *Feminism and Welfare*, p. 93; Lewis, *Women in England*, p. 103.
22 AWCA Syllabus Card 1937.
23 AG 6 April 1937.
24 AWCA Syllabus Card 1937.
25 Koven and Michel in J. Lewis, 'Gender and the family and women's agency in the building of welfare states: the British case', *Social History*, (1994), vol. 19, p. 39.
26 AG, 6 November 1937.
27 AG 6 November 1937.
28 AWCA Minute Book, 23 March 1945.
29 Kingsley Kent, *Gender Reconstruction*, p. 78.
30 Thane, *Women's Participation*, p. 4.
31 AWCA Minute Book 17 January 1939.
32 AWCA Minute Book 15 February 1940.
33 AWCA Minute Book, Annual Report 1939-40.
34 Bruley, *Women in Britain*, p. 105.
35 Bruley, *Women in Britain*, p. 105.
36 AWCA Minute Book 28 August 1939.
37 AWCA Minute Book, Annual Report 1939-40.
38 AWCA Minute Book, 23 December 1941.
39 Jones, *British Public Life*, p. 210.
40 Jones, *British Public Life*, p. 210.
41 Bruley, *Women in Britain*, p. 108.
42 AWCA Minute Book, 21 January 1941.
43 Thane, *Women's Participation*, p. 3.
44 Jones, *British Public Life*, p. 32.
45 AWCA Minute Book, 2 February 1943.
46 AWCA Minute Book, 9 March 1943.
47 Arbroath Town Council Minute Books, 1942-1943, vol. XXIV, A/1/1/46, 17 June 1943.
48 Lewis, *Women in England*, p. 222.
49 SCWCA, Handbook, p. 7.
50 Innes, *Love and Work*, p. 190.
51 AH 8 December 1944; AH 23 February 1945.
52 Thane, *What Difference did the vote make?*, p. 275.
53 AWCA Minute Book, Annual Report 1942-1943.
54 Bruley, *Women in Britain*, p. 85.
55 Arbroath Town Council Minute Books 1942-1943, vol. XXIV, A 1/1/46, 11 February 1943, p. 42.
56 Report of Councillor Mrs A. L. Matthew, Convener of Public Health Committee, 1 October 1946 (A/1/5/54/7).
57 AH 11 February 1944.

[58]   Pugh, *Women's Movement*, p. 59.
[59]   Bruley, *Women in Britain*, p. 275.
[60]   Smith, *British Feminism*, p. 98.

5

'Committee Women'

The Scottish Council of Women Citizens' Association

The AWCA, as was the same for all local branches, were affiliated to the broader Scottish Council, based in Stafford Street, Edinburgh.[1] A National WCA, covering the whole of Britain, was established in 1918, at Caxton Hall in London. This development was paralleled in Scotland a year later, when in 1919 fifteen towns in Scotland, including St Andrews, Greenock and Inverness, saw the need for a distinctive Scottish association and established the SCWCA.[2] The central Scottish council formalised constitutional matters and shaped the activities of local groups. It had a central executive, headed by Honorary Presidents and a President and any resolutions considered had to be seconded by another association before being presented at conference. The pages of the handbook of the SCWCA, which was distributed to all groups, indicates how organisation was a key concept, and one of the reasons the central council gave for joining a WCA was:

> Because a better, happier nation will not be secured by merely wishing for it. *Organisation is necessary*, [my italics] and women, irrespective of differences of politics, religion or education, must unite to form a solid body of opinion.[3]

Much like any large organisation, the SCWCA prepared this handbook to be distributed to every local branch in order that organisational aspects were consistent across the board and throughout all groups. The 1960s version of this handbook firstly details the historical origins of the association, and then lists the constitutional arrangements for the running of WCAs. Of interest is the section on the first fifty years of the WCAs where it was stressed that 'women citizens have extended their work into every field where their efforts can support the rights and improve the conditions of the community in which they live': indicating the SCWCA's civic-mindedness.[4] Meetings of the SCWCA were held in a variety of places during 1931-45, including the Carlyle Hotel in Edinburgh, Mayfield Hostel in Dundee, the Temperance Hotel in Falkirk and MacKay's Tea rooms at Greenock. They held an Annual Business Meeting and a half yearly meeting and continued to meet, mainly in Glasgow and Edinburgh, during the war years indicating their dedication to serving the cause of the WCA.[5] Whilst the SCWCA formalised the activities of local groups it was never dictatorial, preferring members to have autonomy over how their individual groups were run.

Not surprisingly the Scottish association appeared to have been dominated by resolutions from the larger urban areas, especially Glasgow and Edinburgh but also Dundee. This may have reflected the fact that these groups had been in existence much longer than others. The Arbroath group, however, appeared to be one of the few small urban centres who were pro-active in proposing and getting certain resolutions passed. The main campaign during this period, as highlighted in the previous chapter, was for more policewomen. Miss Ann Hampton took this issue to the SCWCA and moved a resolution that 'the Scottish Council of WCA desire to express the urgent need for more policewomen'.[6] Seconded by the Forfar association and after discussion it was approved. Interestingly this was not approved unanimously perhaps indicating some dissent amongst the ranks on this subject.[7] A second campaign, which Ann Hampton brought to the central council, was on the subject of milk and accordingly moved the motion that:

> ... the Scottish Council of Women Citizens
> Associations, believing that a pure milk

supply is of the greatest importance for the health of the Nation, and being convinced that pasteurisation deprives milk of much of its food values, urges the Department of Health to make compulsory the Testing and where necessary the cleaning up of Herds, so that the milk may be distributed pure from the source.[8]

This was passed unanimously and the secretary was then instructed to send a copy to the Secretary of State for Scotland and to the Department of Health – a clear indication that the SCWCA believed their opinion worthy enough for such high government officials. Indeed, in a 1960s version of the SCWCA handbook the campaign to provide stricter hygiene regulations in shops and dairies, and the provision of clean milk, is celebrated as one of the main successes of the SCWCA campaigning history.[9] The roots of this successful campaign can clearly be traced to the Arbroath WCA. Whilst these were the only two resolutions forwarded by the Arbroath association during this time they did second other motions. For example, they were in favour of amending the law of Scotland governing sexual offences against children and young people, and that there should be one ward for maternity cases in every hospital however small.[10] The issue of the provision of maternity beds in hospitals was obviously an issue of much importance to the Arbroath association.

Yet again it appeared to be Ann Hampton who was the main representative for the Arbroath branch at these national meetings. Her name is frequently listed as being in attendance at these meetings and she sat on the Propaganda Committee, and even forwarded herself as a Panel Speaker over two sessions between 1939 and 1941.[11] The SCWCA created these lists of speakers so that local branches could choose from it in order to arrange local meetings and create their lecture syllabus. Each speaker would list what they were prepared to talk on and Ann appeared to concentrate mainly on her travels with talks on Baden-Baden, the Italian Lakes and the Azure Coast. She also included topics on 'A Woman Pioneer in literature' and the 'History of Greek Sculpture'.[12] The mere fact that she was willing to travel and speak on these topics indicates a woman who must have had confidence in public speaking and a willingness to attend local branch meetings anywhere in Scotland. Indeed, the respect Ann Hampton gained within SCWCA circles is clearly illustrated by the fact that she was nominated for the Presidency of the SCWCA in 1934, but opted instead for the Legislation Committee.[13]

The SCWCA was a very important forum for women who were about more than mere 'dreary committee work', however. They aimed to improve the 'status and rights of women in every sphere where anomalies exist' and this included making representations to the Authorities on such issues as the right of a separated, or divorcing wife, to the matrimonial home, the right of a widow to retain the matrimonial home and the right of women to freedom from discriminatory practices in income tax.[14] The perception of women citizens concerning their association is clearly indicated by the inclusion in their handbook of 1943, and quoted from the United Nations Charter, Article 76(c). Their desired aim was clear:

> … to encourage respect for human rights
> and for fundamental freedoms for all
> without distinctions as to race, language,
> sex, or religion, and to encourage
> recognition of the independence of the
> peoples of the world.[15]

In later years the SCWCA contributed to the Scottish Convention of Women in the late 1970s. This was created after International Women's Year in 1975 and included members from groups aligned with the Women's Liberation Movement and went on to campaign for gender parity within the Scottish Parliament.[16] Their representation on this convention indicates the breadth and depth of their work as they were determined to improve the representation of women. It is evident that they 'doggedly pursued equal standing and full representation in otherwise male dominated activities and organisations'.[17]

NOTES

1 The only exception was the Dundee WCA which when it was first established aligned primarily with the National Women Citizens Association in London.
2 SCWCA Handbook, p. 3.
3 SCWCA Handbook, p. 10.
4 SCWCA Handbook, p. 6.
5 Information obtained from SCWCA Minute Books 1919-1944
6 SCWCA Minute Book, 20 March 1943.
7 SCWCA Minute Book, 20 March 1943.
8 SCWCA Minute Book, 3 October 1944.
9 SCWCA Handbook, p. 7.
10 SCWCA Minute Book 24 February 1934; 15 February 1936.
11 SCWCA Minute Book 16 February 1935; 5 November 1938.
12 SCWCA Minute Book 5 November 1938.
13 AWCA Minute Book, 13 December 1934.
14 SCWCA Handbook, p. 6.
15 SCWCA Handbook, Edinburgh, 1943.
16 Innes and Rendall, *Women*, p. 44.
17 Watson, *Daughters of Dundee*, p. 222.

6

Conclusion:
The Politics of Daily Experience[1]

The evidence presented here indicates that the AWCA were undertaking discussions on a range of issues which would not necessarily be instantly associated with them. The success of the AWCA can be seen by the fact that they constantly crossed the line drawn between the genders, enabling them to enter male-dominated areas such as the local Town Council. More importantly, however, they attracted large numbers of women to their cause indicating that there was a genuine need for such a group. There has been a general neglect by historians of the inter-war women's movement to actually investigate or even consult the archives of these groups. Perhaps this is because the primary source material are dispersed widely across the country and there is no central archive for this collection. Indeed, many papers and documents remain in private hands - as is the case with the Arbroath WCA papers – which renders the task of research that much harder. Irrespective of problems with sources, however, the analysis of the work of the WCAs also suffers from an historical approach to the study of the women's movement that places far too much emphasis on prescriptive labels such as 'new' and 'old' feminism. As Sue Innes has argued 'the division of 'old' and 'new' feminisms after 1918 mapped onto the binary of equality and difference, was not necessarily a tension for women's organisations.'[2] Historians' criticisms of new feminists have led to a general assertion that such groups simply ignored equality issues. It is clear from the evidence presented here that the AWCA were a dynamic women's group which incorporated both elements of new or welfare feminism, and also that of the equal rights tradition. It has been shown, therefore, that the work of groups such as the AWCA does not fit easily into these historical distinctions. It is clear that the

AWCA were not only effective campaigners on such issues as welfare provisions, but they were also to the fore in the campaign for more policewomen and greater female participation in local government.

It is also true that historical research has become somewhat fixated with distinctions of feminism and that as a result the work of organisations such as the AWCA has come to be portrayed as nothing more than 'dreary committee work'.[3] In order to move away from any sort of pre-judgement on a feminist scale, the evidence of these groups should be considered from the perspective that they in fact provided an important space for women to exchange political ideas and learn from other women involved in politics. These developments in gender theory towards a broader concept of political discourse have obviously enabled historians to re-assess the work of groups such as the AWCA in a more meaningful way. As Hunt has argued the importance of these groups came down to the fact that entrance into formal politics was difficult for women to achieve, and thus it was the 'politics that sprang from daily experience … that women found ways to conceive of themselves as political actors'.[4] This was aided and encouraged by the highly organised structures of the WCAs and this helped to instil a great sense of comradeship in women and which in many cases broke the isolation and loneliness felt by many women in rural and urban Scotland. The WCA trained women in minute-taking and how to chair meetings, and gave them the confidence to undertake such tasks as public speaking. It can be no coincidence that after having received such training and tuition that many women felt able and confident enough to put themselves forward for elections to public office, particularly at the local level. Indeed, even those who were not as timid, groups such as the WCA provided an outlet for women who were thought of as more able and who may have ended up frustrated at the limitations placed on them in their wider social circles. They also created networks, and gave opportunities for their members to escape their normal surroundings to places such as Edinburgh and London. This is a process of politicisation and it was an introduction to formal organisational structures and its importance cannot be underestimated.

The AWCA can legitimately be viewed as an active women's group, indeed, on many occasions a very pro-active group, which functioned at a time when most historians believed the women's movement had fallen into inexorable decline. Indeed, the evidence presented here supports the findings of Innes and Norman Watson who questioned this, indicating that during the inter-war years and beyond that female political campaigning did not come to an abrupt halt. It is interesting to consider why this misconception has endured and the reasons are varied. But pivotal in this development appears to be an over-reliance on evidence gathered from the operations of groups such as the NUSEC in chronicling the story of the inter-war women's movement. Indeed, the mere fact that these groups have been overlooked by historians remains a worrying problem, and that the historical framework that underpins the study of women's political activities needs to be re-explored. One way forward could be to examine the concept that there were different waves of feminism in as much as women's political activities are often described in terms of first or second wave feminism: the first was the era of the suffragette movement and the second encompassing the work of the WLM. This has led to an over-concentration on the activities of these movements. In contrast, groups such as the AWCA are excluded from this rigid framework, and because they were perceived as dull and dreary that this orthodoxy denied the women involved in these groups their place in history and their part in the historical process. Only by moving away from this framework and exploring the archives of groups such as the AWCA will the campaigns for equality of opportunity be understood more fully, thus leading to a fairer and more representative history.

The research here has demonstrated that historians' neglect of groups such as the WCAs has directly led to a misjudgement of the women's movement during this period, and has highlighted the common misconception that female political campaigning ceased in 1928. Importantly, this study has met two further objectives; that of preserving the archive of the AWCA, and in the second case bringing the important work and history of this local group to public attention, while moving the parameters of this research field into gender away from large urban areas to smaller ones. It is vital for a more balanced national picture that areas such as Angus are not overshadowed by their larger neighbours and thus written out of the historical record. Having stated all of this, however, by highlighting the existence of the AWCA this research gives a clear indication of the continued political activities of women after 1928, and in so doing challenges the orthodox historical gender stereotype while at the same advancing a more positive role for women in developing civil society during the period 1931 to 1945.

NOTES

1. Taken from Hunt, *Women as Citizens*, p. 249.
2. Innes, Constructing Women's Citizenship, p. 621.
3. Holdsworth, *Out of the Doll's House*, p. 191.
4. Hunt, *Women as Citizens*, p. 249.

Epilogue

Personal Reflections

I

'What the WCA has meant to me'

I can hardly believe that it is over fifty years since I joined the Arbroath branch of the then Scottish Women Citizens' Association. When I was young, most married women stayed at home and domesticity was their life, except perhaps if they had a sporting interest. It was a chance remark by a friend that took me to my first meeting and to my amazement there was a company of about one hundred and fifty women present. I listened with great interest to the female speakers and realised that this was not just 'a cup of tea and a chat' meeting.

In due course I became a committee member of the Arbroath Women Citizens' Association, progressing to the post of Secretary and finally President. It was through meeting some very dedicated women at the North East District, which included Dundee, Aberdeen and St Andrews, which inspired me to become involved in civic projects. So many subjects were covered and to our everlasting credit Arbroath put forward a motion to the Legislative Committee, which eventually resulted in the Succession (Scotland) Act 1964, to the benefit of all widows.

Joining the Women Citizens Association opened up a new world of civic awareness and interest for me. As a spin-off we opened a club for women, called the Lochlands Club, and Citizens members made and served tea each week to elderly ladies whilst also providing entertainment. This was a happy affair. I do not remember any friction of any kind.

As time went by I developed an interest in public speaking and the presentation skills which go with it, so much so that I stood at the local elections as an Independent candidate and, with the help of willing citizens, took a council seat in a traditionally Labour ward.

There is no explanation as to why membership started to dwindle but gradually things became so bad that one after another clubs folded, until we in Arbroath became the solitary survivor. Once again I was voted by the Committee to serve as President, so my pride in being a member was again boosted.

It is difficult to put into words what the Women Citizens has meant to me. It gave me an insight into civic rights and wrongs, a desire to do something to help our local community. It was a way to make friends and in many ways it changed my life, helping me to realise potential which I did not know I had. I was involved in helping others in many, many ways. I owe a debt of gratitude to the Association for moulding my life, and am happy to continue to be an active member.

Caroline H. Florence
Longest-serving 'woman citizen' in Arbroath
January 2007

II

The importance of the AWCA becomes immediately apparent when it is considered that they are believed to be the last association in existence in Scotland today. To have lasted for over seventy-five years is an accomplishment in itself, but to be the last out of an original twenty WCAs is a quite remarkable achievement. The present-day AWCA is not as political as it once was, but it is still an important forum for bringing women together. In fact, today they still have approximately thirty-five members and are therefore not lacking in support. Their main concern, like many associations, is that young members are not attracted to their cause and it is sad to say that when this generation of AWCA women are gone there may be no-one left to broadcast the message of citizenship.

Whilst not as politically active, they still have a voice on certain issues. For example, they succeeded in convincing the Town Council of the need for a light beside Webster Theatre to enable pedestrians to use the path at night. They also wrote to the Dundee *Courier*, expressing their dismay at the cost of the Scottish Parliament building. Nowadays, however, they generally arrange lectures by speakers of interest and organise more social events. It is not clear why the AWCA have outlived all the other associations for they were never the most affluent and always struggling to survive financially. What is evident is that as the last WCA in existence it is up to historians to make sure that, unlike so many women's groups of their time, they do not become hidden from history. This publication ensures that their story is not lost to posterity.

Sarah Browne
March 2007

Appendix I: Presidents of the AWCA*

1931	Mrs Corsar**
1931-1933	Mrs Harley
1933-1934	Miss Ann Hampton
1934-1935	Mrs W. F. Anderson
1935-1936	Mrs Matthew
1936-1938	Mrs Patterson
1938-1939	Mrs McCrae Wilson
1939-1940	Mrs Patterson
1940-1941	Mrs McCrae Wilson
1941-1943	Miss Helen Hampton
1943-1945	Mrs D. R. MacDonald
1944	Mrs Glen

* After a rather unorganised beginning due to circumstances such as Mrs Corsar's death, Presidents began to take office every March from 1934 onwards and followed this pattern right through the period.

** Mrs Corsar was only president from February until September 1931 as she died in September.

Appendix II: Committees 1931-1945

1931-1932

President:	Mrs Corsar
Vice President:	Miss Hampton
Honorary Treasurer:	Mrs Craig
Honorary Secretary:	Mrs Freeman
Committee:	Mrs A. C. Anderson, Mrs T. S. Anderson, Mrs Greig, Mrs J. Joss, Mrs J. Matthew, Mrs G. S. Robertson, Mrs W. H. Thorneycroft.

Subdivided into groups with remit to examine the Infirmary, Letting of Halls, the Cinema and Housing.

1932-1933

President:	Mrs Harley
Vice President:	Miss Hampton
Honorary Treasurer:	Mrs Garvie and Mrs Patterson
Honorary Secretary:	n/a
Committee:	Mrs A. C. Anderson, Mrs J. S. Anderson, Mrs W. F. Anderson, Mrs Joss, Mrs Matthew, Mrs Thorneycroft, Mrs A. K. Adamson, Miss Chisholm, Mrs Lamb, Miss Mann, Mrs Phillips and Mrs A. L. Robertson.

Subdivided into groups with remit to examine the Cinema, Probation, Housing and Health Visits.

1933-1934

Honorary President:	Mrs Harley
President:	Miss Ann Hampton
Vice Presidents:	Mrs W. F. Anderson and Mrs Matthew
Joint Treasurers:	Mrs Patterson and Mrs Garvie
Joint Secretaries:	Mrs Freeman and Mrs J. S. Anderson
Committee:	Mrs A. C. Anderson, Mrs. A. K. Adamson, Miss Chisholm, Mrs Joss, Mrs Lamb, Mrs Phillips, Mrs G. L. Robertson, Mrs Thorneycroft, Miss Beattie, Mrs Bennett, Miss Duncan, Miss Ellis.

Subdivided into groups with remit to examine the Infirmary, the Cinema, Health Visits and Housing.

1934-1935

Honorary Presidents:	Mrs Harley and Miss Hampton
President:	Mrs W. F. Anderson
Vice Presidents:	Mrs Matthew and Mrs Garvie
Treasurer:	Mrs Patterson
Secretaries:	Mrs J. S. Anderson and Miss Ellis
Committee:	Mrs A. K. Adamson, Miss Beattie, Miss M. Chisholm, Miss Duncan, Mrs Joss, Mrs Freeman, Mrs Macara, Mrs D. Byars, Mrs McCrae Wilson and Mrs Wilkie.

Subdivided into groups with remit to examine the Infirmary, the Cinema, Housing and Entertainment.

1935-1936

Honorary Presidents: Mrs Harley and Miss Hampton

President: Mrs Matthew

Vice Presidents: Mrs Patterson and Mrs Wilson

Secretaries: Mrs T. S. Anderson and Miss Ellis

Treasurers: Mrs Garvie and Mrs Bennett

Committee: Miss Macara, Mrs Byars, Mrs Wilkie, Miss Chisholm, Mrs Davidson, Mrs W. F. Anderson, Mrs Cope, Mrs Fleming, Miss Low and Miss Finlayson.

Subdivided into groups with remit to examine Housing, the Cinema, Mental Deficiency, Probation and Child Welfare, Entertainment and the AWCA Syllabus.

1936-1937

Honorary Presidents: Mrs Harley and Miss Hampton

President: Mrs Patterson

Vice Presidents: Mrs Wilson and Mrs McAra

Secretary: Mrs Wilkie

Treasurers: Mrs Garvie and Mrs Bennett

Committee: Mrs J. Anderson, Miss Mather, Mrs A. C. Anderson, Mrs W. F. Anderson, Mrs T. S. Anderson, Mrs D. Byars, Mrs Cope, Mrs Donald, Mrs Fleming, Mrs Matthew, Miss Finalyson and Miss Low.

Subdivided into groups with remit to examine Entertainment, Mental Deficiency, Maternity, the Cinema, Housing and the AWCA Syllabus.

1937-1938

Honorary Presidents:	Mrs Harley and Miss Hampton
President:	Mrs Patterson
Vice Presidents:	Mrs McCrae Wilson and Mrs Matthew
Secretary:	Mrs Wilkie
Treasurer:	Mrs Garvie
Committee:	Mrs J. Anderson, Mrs. T. S. Anderson, Mrs Donald, Mrs Bennett, Mrs McAra, Mrs Cope, Miss Mather, Mrs D. R. McDonald, Mrs G. S. Robertson, Mrs Milne, Mrs McNair, Mrs Smith, Mrs Ferrier, Miss Watson.

Subdivided into groups with remit to examine Entertainment, Maternity, the Cinema, Vagrancy, Housing and the AWCA Syllabus.

1938-1939

Honorary Presidents:	Mrs Harley and Miss Hampton
President:	Mrs McCrae Wilson
Vice President:	Miss K. Mather
Secretary:	Mrs Matthew
Treasurer:	Mrs Ferrier
Committee:	Mrs T. S. Anderson, Mrs Jas. Anderson, Mrs Cope, Mrs McDonald, Mrs G. S. Robertson, Mrs Smith, Miss Watson, Mrs Patterson, Mrs Wilkie, Mrs McCowat, Mrs Murray and Mrs Byars.

Subdivided into groups with remit to examine Entertainment, Maternity, the Cinema, Vagrancy and Probation, Housing, Country Dancing, the Endowment Fund and the AWCA Syllabus.

1939-1940

President:	Mrs Patterson
Vice President:	Mrs McCrae Wilson
Secretary:	Mrs McCowat
Treasurer:	Mrs James Anderson
Committee:	Mrs Ferrier, Mrs D. R. McDonald, Mrs T. S. Anderson, Mrs Smith, Mrs G. S. Robertson, Mrs David Cargill, Mrs Glen, Mrs McDowal, Mrs Pirie, Mrs James Law, Mrs A. T. Myles, Miss D. M. Robertson.

Subdivided into groups with remit to examine Entertainment, the Endowment Fund and Probation.

1940-1941

Honorary Presidents:	Mrs Harley and Miss Hampton
President:	Mrs McCrae Wilson
Vice Presidents:	Mrs D. R. MacDonald, Mrs McDowall and Miss H. Hampton
Secretaries:	Mrs McCowat and Mrs Glen
Treasurers:	Mrs J. Anderson and Mrs Pirie
Committee:	Mrs Patterson, Mrs Ferrier, Mrs J. S. Anderson, Mrs G. S. Robertson, Mrs D. Cargill, Mrs A. S. Myles, Miss D. M. Robertson, Miss E. Sim, Mrs Savage, Mrs Mollinson and Miss Bonnyman.

Subdivided into groups with remit to examine Maternity, Savings, WVS, the Red Cross, Social, Work Parties and Wool and Sewing.

1941-1942

Honorary Presidents:	Mrs Harley and Miss Hampton
President:	Miss Helen Hampton
Vice Presidents:	Mrs D. R. MacDonald and Mrs McDowall
Secretaries:	Mrs McCowat and Mrs Glen
Treasurers:	Mrs James Anderson and Mrs D. Cargill
Committee:	Mrs McCrae Wilson, Mrs J. Patterson, Mrs T. S. Anderson, Mrs G. S. Robertson, Miss D. M. Robertson, Miss E. Sim, Mrs Savage, Mrs Mollison, Miss Ure, Miss Bonnyman, Mrs Robertson, Mrs Byars.

Subdivided into groups with remit to examine Entertainment and Wool.

1942-1943

Honorary President:	Mrs Harley and Miss Hampton
President:	Miss Helen Hampton
Vice President:	Mrs D. R. MacDonald and Mrs Glen
Secretaries:	Mrs McCowat and Miss Ure
Treasurers:	Mrs James Anderson and Miss Bonnyman
Committee:	Mrs McCrae Wilson, Mrs John Patterson, Mrs J. S. Anderson, Mrs G. S. Robertson, Miss E. Sim, Mrs Byars, Mrs Ferrier, Mrs Robertson, Mrs F. W. Ferguson, Mrs Geo. Watson, Mrs Gardner, Mrs Kirkcaldy, Miss Fairweather, Miss Smith.

Subdivided into groups with remit to examine Entertainment, Wool and Savings.

1943-1944

Honorary President:	Mrs Harley and Miss Hampton
President:	Mrs D. R. MacDonald
Vice Presidents:	Mrs Glen, Miss Ure, Mrs J. S. Anderson
Secretary:	Mrs McCowat
Treasurers:	Mrs James Anderson and Miss Bonnyman
Committee:	Councillor Mrs McCrae Wilson, Mrs John Patterson, Mrs G. S. Robertson, Miss E. Sim, Mrs Byars, Mrs Robertson, Mrs J. W. Ferguson, Mrs Geo. Watson, Mrs Kirkcaldy, Mrs Gardner, Miss Smith, Miss Fairweather, Miss H. Hampton, Councillor Mrs John Matthew.

1944-1945

Honorary President:	Mrs Harley and Miss Hampton
President:	Mrs D. R. MacDonald
Vice President:	Mrs Glen
Secretary:	Mrs Petty
Treasurer:	Miss Bonnyman
Committee:	Mrs Jas. Anderson, Miss Anderson, Miss Byars, Miss Ducat, Miss Fairweather, Mrs Gardner, Miss H. Hampton, Mrs Ferguson, Councillor Mrs John Matthew, Mrs Mollison, Mrs John Patterson, Mrs G. S. Robertson, Miss Smith, Councillor Mrs McCrae Wilson, Mrs E. Robertson.

Subdivided into groups with remit to examine Entertainment, Wool and Savings.

Bibliography

Unpublished Primary Sources

Angus Archives

A/1/1/46 Arbroath Town Council Minute Books 1942-1943 vol. xxiv

A/1/5/54/7 Report of Councillor Mrs A.L. Matthew, Convener of the Public Health Committee 1 October 1946.

National Archives of Scotland

GD1/1076/5 Scottish Council of Women Citizens Associations Minute Book 1919-1932

GD1/1076/6 Scottish Council of Women Citizens Associations Minute Book 1932-1944

GD1/1076/7 Scottish Council of Women Citizens Associations Minute Book 1944-1956

Private Archive, Arbroath

Arbroath Women Citizens' Association (minute books 1931-1945, syllabus cards, 1931-1950).

University of Dundee Archive Services

THB 20/17 Minute book of the Arbroath Infirmary Board Meetings January 1931-30 November 1932

THB 20/19-22 Minute book of the Arbroath Infirmary Board Meetings 22 March 1939 – 18 December 1940.

Published Primary Sources

Blair, C., *Rural Journey – A History of the SWRI – From Cradle to Majority*, (Edinburgh, 1940).

Strachey, R., *The Cause: A Short History of the Women's Movement in Great Britain*, (London, 1928).

Secondary Sources

Abrams, L., 'Introduction: Gendering the Agenda' in L. Abrams, E. Gordon, D. Simonton and E. Yeo (eds), *Gender in Scottish History Since 1700*, (Edinburgh, 2006).

Adam, I. H., *The Making of Urban Scotland*, (Montreal, 1978).

Alberti, J., *Beyond Suffrage: Feminists in War and Peace 1914-1928*, (London, 1989).

Banks, O., *Faces of Feminism – A Study of Feminism as a Social Movement*, (Oxford, 1987).

Banks, O., *The Politics of British Feminism 1918-1970*, (Aldershot, 1993).

Beaumont, C., 'The Women's Movement, Politics and Citizenship 1918-1950s' in I. Zweiniger-Bargielowska (ed), *Women in Twentieth Century Britain*, (Harlow, 2001).

Beddoe, D., *Back to Home and Duty: Women Between the Wars 1918-1939*, (London, 1989).

Breitenbach, E. and Gordon, E., *Out of Bounds: Women in Scottish Society 1880-1945*, (Edinburgh, 1992).

Bruley, S., *Women in Britain Since 1900*, (London, 1999).

Bryson, V., *Feminist Political Theory – An Introduction*, (London, 1992).

Caine, B., *English Feminism, 1780-1980*, (Oxford, 1997).

Ewan, E. and Meikle, M. 'Introduction' in E. Ewan and M. M. Meikle (eds), *Women in Scotland c. 1100 – 1750*, (East Linton, 1999).

Hall, D. V., *Making Things Happen: A History of the first 25 years of the Federation*, (London, 1963).

Harrison, B., *Prudent Revolutionaries – Portraits of British Feminists During the Wars*, (Oxford, 1987).

Hendry, J., 'Snug in the Asylum of Taciturnity: Women's History in Scotland' in I. Donnachie and C. A. Whatley (eds), *The Manufacture of Scottish History*, (Edinburgh, 1992).

Holdsworth, A., *Out of the Doll's House: The Story of Women in the Twentieth Century*, (London, 1989).

Hunt, K., 'Women as Citizens: Changing the Polity' in D. Simonton (ed), *The Routledge History of Women in Europe Since 1700*, (Abingdon, 2006).

Innes, S., 'Preface' in L. Leneman, *Into the Foreground – A Century of Scottish Women in Photographs*, (Edinburgh, 1993).

Innes, S., and Rendall, J., 'Women, Gender and Politics' in L. Abrams, E. Gordon, D. Simonton and E. Yeo (eds), *Gender in Scottish History Since 1700*, (Edinburgh, 2006).

Jones, H., *Women in British Public Life 1914-1950: Gender, Power and Social Policy*, (Harlow, 2000).

King, E., *The Scottish Women's Suffrage Movement*, (Glasgow, 1978).

King, E., 'The Scottish Women's Suffrage Movement' in E. Breitenbach and E. Gordon (eds), *Out of Bounds: Women in Scottish Society 1880-1945*, (Edinburgh, 1992).

Kingsley Kent, S., *Gender and Power in Britain 1640-1990*, (London, 1999).

Kingsley Kent, S., 'Gender Reconstruction after the First World War' in H.L Smith (ed), *British Feminism in the Twentieth Century*, (Aldershot, 1990).

Leneman, L., *A Guid Cause: The Women's Suffrage Movement in Scotland*, (Edinburgh, 1995).

Leneman, L., 'Dundee and the Women's Suffrage Movement 1907-

1914' in C. A. Whatley, *The Remaking of Juteopolis – Dundee circa 1891-1991*, (Dundee, 1992).

Lewis, J., 'Feminism and Welfare' in J. Mitchell and A. Oakley (eds), *What is Feminism?*, (Oxford, 1986).

Lewis, J., *Women in England 1870-1950 – Sexual Division and Social Change*, (Sussex, 1984).

McDermid, J., 'Missing Persons? Women in Scottish History' in T. Brothersone, D. Simonton and O. Walsh (eds), *Gendering Scottish History – An International Approach*, (Glasgow, 1999).

Pugh, M. 'Domesticity and the Decline of Feminism, 1930-1950' in H. L. Smith, *British Feminism in the Twentieth Century*, (Aldershot, 1990).

Pugh, M., *Women and the Women's Movement in Britain 1914-1999*, (London, 2000).

Smith, H. L., 'British Feminism in the 1920s' in H. L. Smith, *British Feminism in the Twentieth Century*, (Aldershot, 1990).

Spender, D., *There's Always Been a Women's Movement this Century*, (London, 1983).

Spring Rice, M., *Working Class Wives: Their Health and Conditions*, (London, 1979).

Turner, W. H. K., *The Textile Industry of Arbroath since the early 18th Century*, (Dundee, 1954).

Journal Articles

Beaumont, C., 'Citizens Not Feminists: The Boundary Negotiated Between Citizenship and Feminism By Mainstream Women's Organizations in England, 1928-1939', *Women's History Review*, vol. 9, 2000.

Innes, S., 'Constructing Women's Citizenship in the Interwar Period: The Edinburgh Women Citizens Association, *Women's History Review*, vol. 13, November 2004.

Lewis, J., 'Gender and the family and women's agency in the building of welfare states: The British case', *Social History*, (1994), vol. 19.

Thane, P., 'What Difference did the Vote Make?' Women in Public and Private Life in Britain since 1918', *Historical Research*, vol. 76, no. 192, May 2003.

Thane, P., 'Women's Participation in Political and Public Life: Building on Past Experience. What has changed and why since women got the vote?', *Women and Equality Unit*, December, 2003.

Theses

Innes, S., 'Love and Work: Feminism, Family and Ideas of Equality and Citizenship: Britain 1900-1939', (unpublished Ph.D thesis, University of Edinburgh, 1998).

Watson, N., 'Daughters of Dundee – Gender and Politics in Dundee – The Representation of Women 1870-1977' (unpublished Ph.D thesis, Open University, 2000).

Periodicals

The Arbroath Yearbook and Eastern Angus Directory

The Forfar Directory

Newspapers

The Arbroath Guide

The Arbroath Herald

The Forfar Dispatch

The Forfar Herald

The Scotsman

Pamphlets

Scottish Council of Women Citizens' Associations, *Handbook*, (Edinburgh, 1948).

Scottish Council of Women Citizens' Associations, *Handbook*, (Edinburgh, undated but probably c. 1968).

Unpublished

Florence, C. H., *The History of the Scottish Women's Association and the Arbroath Women's Association, 1931-2003*, (unpublished manuscript, 2003).

Index

Aberdeen .... p. 10

Aid to Russia Fund .... p. 46

anti-feminism .... p. 16

Arbroath .... p. 5, 9, 10, 11, 12, 20, 47

Arbroath Infirmary .... p. 24, 41, 45

    Campaign for Maternity bed .... p. 29, 43, 45, 53

Arbroath Town Council .... p. 29, 48, 57, 62

Billington Greig, Teresa .... p. 10

Brechin .... p. 10, 25

Breitenbach, Esther .... p. 3

British Women's Temperance Association .... p. 12, 20

Business and Professional Women's Group .... p. 18, 20

Campbell-Bannerman, Henry .... p. 10

Carnoustie .... p. 10

Caxton Hall, London .... p. 11, 52

Corsar, Mrs .... p. 26

Crooker, Miss .... p. 10

Despard, Charlotte .... p. 11

Drummond, Flora .... p. 10

Dugdale, Una .... p. 10, 12

Duncan, Miss F. M. .... p. 11

Duncan, Mrs .... p. 11

Dundee .... p. 9, 43

equal pay .... p. 47

Forfar .... p. 10, 11, 12

Fraser, Helen .... p. 10, 12

Gawthorpe, Miss .... p. 10

Gordon, Eleanor .... p. 3

Hampton, Ann .... p. 26, 27, 43, 46, 47, 53, 54, 55

Hampton, Helen .... p. 27, 28

Holloway Prison .... p. 11

Indian Women's Franchise .... p. 42

Innes, Sue .... p. 1, 4, 5, 9, 28, 29, 41, 57, 59

King, Elspeth .... p. 12, 20

Kinnettles .... p. 11

Kirriemuir .... p. 10

labour movement .... p. 29

Leneman, Leah .... p. 3, 9

MacKenzie, Lady Leslie .... p. 23

McCrae Wilson, Mrs.. p. 28, 48

Marshall, R. K. .... p. 3

Matthew, Mrs .... p. 28, 47, 48

Montrose .... p. 9, 10

Munro, Anna .... p. 11, 12

New, Edith .... p. 12

new feminism.. p. 3, 4, 16, 43, 45, 57

North-East Area of Women Citizens' Associations................................. p. 25

nursery schools .... p. 44, 45

Pankhurst, Mrs... p. 10

Paul, Alice .... p. 12

Perthshire .... p. 10

policewomen .... p. 46, 53

political spaces .... p. 2, 15, 58

pure milk campaign .... p. 53

Rathbone, Eleanor .... p. 17, 18, 19, 42

Robinson, Annott... p. 11

Sanderson, Amy... p. 11

Scottish Convention of Women... p. 55

Scottish Council of Women Citizens' Association Handbook......... pp. 52-53

Strachey, Ray .... p. 1, 7

Suffrage Campaign

    National Union of Societies for Equal Citizenship .... p. 17, 49, 59

National Union of Women's Suffrage Societies .... p. 10, 17, 18

Women's Freedom League .... p. 10, 11, 17

Women's Social and Political Union .... p. 10, 11, 12

Suffragettes .... p. 2, 10, 11, 12, 59

Townswomen's Guilds .... p. 18

Watson, Norman .... p. 4, 5, 9, 28, 41, 59

welfare feminism .... p. 25, 42, 43, 48, 57

Women Citizens' Association

    Dundee Branch.. p. 5, 9, 19, 23, 25, 28, 29, 42

    Edinburgh Branch .... p. 3, 4, 5, 9, 19, 27, 28, 29

    Forfar Branch.. p. 19, 23, 25, 29, 47, 53

    Scottish Council of............................... p. 7, 19, 23, 25, 26, 46, 47, pp. 52-55

Women Citizens' Association aims... p. 24

Women's Co-operative Guild .... p. 20, 29

Women's Health Enquiry .... p. 21, 42

Women's Institutes .... p. 18

Women's Liberation Movement... p. 2, 53, 59

Women's movement

    Division of... pp. 16-17, p. 20

    Fragmentation of.. pp. 17-18, p. 20

Women's Rural Institutes .... p. 18, 20

Women's Voluntary Service.. p. 43

Work parties .... p. 42

Young Women's Christian Association .... p. 12

The Abertay Historical Society

Honorary Presidents
Lord Provost of the City of Dundee
Principal of the University of Dundee
Principal of the University of St Andrews

President
Richard Cullen

Vice-President
Jan Merchant

General Secretary
Matthew Jarron
c/o University of Dundee Museum Services, Dundee DD1 4HN
e-mail: museum@dundee.ac.uk

Treasurer
Charlotte Lythe
90 Dundee Road, Broughty Ferry, Dundee DD5 1DW
e-mail: c.lythe1@btinternet.com

Book Editor
Billy Kenefick
History, School of Humanities, University of Dundee,
Dundee DD1 4HN

Sales Secretary
Catherine Smith
SUAT, 55 South Methven Street, Perth PH1 5NX
e-mail: csmith@suat.co.uk

The Society was founded in May 1947 and exists to promote interest
in local history. For further information, please visit our website at
www.abertay.org.uk

Publications of the Abertay Historical Society currently in print

No.28 Enid Gauldie, *One Artful and Ambitious Individual, Alexander Riddoch (1745-1822), (Provost of Dundee 1787-1819)*. (1989) ISBN 0 900019 24 7

No.35 Annette M. Smith, *The Nine Trades of Dundee*. (1995) ISBN 0 900019 31 X

No.37 Michael St John, *The Demands of the People, Dundee Radicalism 1850-1870*. (1997) ISBN 0 900019 33 6

No.38 W.M. Mathew, *Keiller's of Dundee, The Rise of the Marmalade Dynasty 1800-1879*. (1998) ISBN 0 900019 35 2

No.39 Lorraine Walsh, *Patrons, Poverty & profit: Organised Charity in Nineteenth Century Dundee*. (2000) ISBN 0 900019 35 2

No.41 Ian McCraw, *Victorian Dundee at Worship*. (2002) ISBN 0 900019 37 9

No.42 Andrew Murray Scott, *Dundee's Literary Lives vol 1: Fifteenth to Nineteenth Century*. (2003) ISBN 0 900019 38 7

No 43 Andrew Murray Scott, *Dundee's Literary Lives vol 2: Twentieth Century* (2004) ISBN 0 900019 39 5

No 45 Annette M. Smith, *The Guildry of Dundee: A History of the Merchant Guild of Dundee up to the 19th century*. (2005) ISBN 0 900019 42 5

No 46 Mary Verschuur, *A Noble and Potent Lady: Katherine Campbell, Countess of Crawford*. (2006) ISBN 0 900019 43 3

No 47 Kenneth Cameron, *The Schoolmaster Engineer: Adam Anderson of Perth & St Andrews 1780-1846*. (2007) ISBN 0 900019 44 1

All publications may be obtained through booksellers or by post from the Hon Sales Secretary, Abertay Historical Society, SUAT, 55 South Methven Street, Perth, PH1 5NX (e-mail: csmith@suat.co.uk)